SUPERNATURAL
STEAM

by J. A. BROOKS

JARROLD

About the author

John Brooks has had a lifelong interest in the supernatural, particularly the way ghost stories complement and enhance history. This is his second collection of ghost stories with a railway background, following the successful *Railway Ghosts*. He has also written accounts of the ghosts of Wales, the Cotswolds, London and the Lake District, and is the author of *Britain's Haunted Heritage*, a comprehensive study of hauntings throughout the country. Born in Cambridge in 1939, he lives in the depths of Norfolk with a wife, children and animals.

Acknowledgements

The author and publishers are grateful to all who gave help and advice, particularly members of the various preservation societies. The suggestions of Philip Atkins of the National Railway Museum were valuable in tracing illustrations, while Peter Owen Jones's paintings are magnificent in evoking the drama and beauty of the steam era, even though (apart from the cover) they are reproduced here in black and white.

Picture credits

Imperial War Museum: p.102; Jarrold Publishing: pages 21, 32, 53, 68, 73, 74, 76, 78, 81, 85, 118, 122, 123; John C. N. Whitwam: p.95; Main Line Steam Trust (photographer John East): p.58; National Portrait Gallery: p.108; National Railway Museum, York: pages 16, 23, 35, 47, 49, 57, 65, 77, 91, 100, 104-5; North Norfolk Railway: p.39; Peter Owen Jones: cover; pages 6-7, 10-11, 26-27, 30, 42, 62, 88, 114-5, 127; The Harbour Inne, Arley: p.111

ISBN 0-7117-0593-3
© 1992 Jarrold Publishing

Printed in Great Britain by
Jarrold Printing, Norwich. 1/92

Contents

'*Autumn at Ais Gill*'

Introduction

All of these twelve stories have steam railways as their background. In all cases except one they feature settings where there are preserved lines today. The exception uses that mecca of steam enthusiasts, the Settle and Carlisle line. The tales derive from different periods in railway history, from the mid-Victorian era to the present day, and historical events and characters feature in several of them, as do real (if you believe in such things) ghosts.

Every effort has been made to ensure accuracy, especially in regard to the running of the railways of the time. Where preserved railways have a role in the stories their administrators have been offered the opportunity of commenting on them. Thus the Strathspey pointed out that given normal working practice the events described at Aviemore in 'The Red Dawn' would have been unlikely. However, it was wartime, and an author must be allowed some licence.

Historical characters feature in three of the stories – Torry and Mickle in 'Retribution', Caudle, Follows and Nicholson in 'The Black Crow', and Lord Kitchener in 'The Red Dawn'. All others are fictitious and bear no intentional resemblance to anyone living, today or in the past. After my last collection of short stories about railways, *Railway Ghosts*, a lady wrote to say she lived in a house described in one of the stories, and how had I known of the tragedy which caused it to be haunted! I wonder whether any of these tales will conjure a similar response.

Uncle Ben

We children were looking forward to Friday the thirteenth. What spectacular disaster would it bring? Would the train smash through the terminus buffers or its boiler explode? Could it be that the two signalmen at Corfe and Swanage would send out trains on the same track? No, the calamity was much more subtle. Friday the thirteenth saw the arrival of Uncle Ben.

Looking at him, you'd first have thought him to be an absent-minded parson or professor. He had a lovely face, full of kindness, and a gentle nature which brought him love from children as well as animals. In later years Roald Dahl's *BFG* became a favourite book with my grandchildren. Uncle Ben often looked, and frequently behaved, like Dahl's famous Big Friendly Giant.

He was my father's elder brother. As such, Ben had worked at the family's Derbyshire farm (where they were tenants) while Father left to seek his fortune elsewhere, ending up on the railways as a passenger guard working out of Salisbury on the London and South Western Railway. Just before the outbreak of the First World War he married my mother, his childhood sweetheart, and I was conceived soon after.

Father might have decided to work on the railway throughout the war but instead he soon volunteered for the army and fought at Gallipoli. He left the army, unscathed, in 1919 and reapplied for his old job, to which he was entitled. Instead the company offered him the post of stationmaster at Corfe Castle in Dorset, on the Wareham to Swanage branchline. Although reluctant to accept this change at first, he soon realised the advantages (the pleasures of living in the country and the excellent accommodation for his ever-growing family) and settled down happily enough. Meanwhile in Derbyshire Uncle Ben was finding it more and more difficult to pay the rent owed on the farm.

After a couple of years the post of stationmaster became vacant at Swanage. Father applied and was pleasantly surprised when he was appointed.

'The Midland Way South' – a Compound at Armathwaite

The post carried not only more extensive duties but also considerable status in a town still expanding as a holiday resort. Father soon became a respected figure in Swanage, and the station was very busy on Saturdays in summer when there were nearly thirty passenger-train arrivals each day. Even on the quietest of winter weekdays there were a handful of passengers to deal with, as well as the parcels office and goods yard to run. About a dozen staff came under Father's command, and we children were usually on pretty good terms with all of them, though their patience must have been sorely tried at times by our mischief.

We had planned an especially wicked escapade for Friday the thirteenth. Some time before we had hidden a milk churn and then steadily filled it with sand. When the time came the combined strength of the five of us was just enough to get it onto a platform trolley with several empties. We then placed this in the usual position to wait for the milk van on the afternoon goods. We hoped that the immovable churn would bring us a laugh at the expense of Joe Gatting, the junior porter who was our current enemy.

In fact the prank ended disastrously. Father told Joe to get the trolley moved to the goods shed. When he tried to do so, the unexpected weight of the sand-filled churn caused him to lose control on the platform ramp. The trolley ran away, crashing into point-rodding and signal wires and emptying its load, including the sand, onto the tracks. It was in the middle of the furore following this that Uncle Ben arrived on the 4.40 from Bournemouth Central.

Normally we only saw Uncle Ben once a year unless there was a family wedding or funeral. Our annual visit to Derbyshire was possible thanks to the cheap tickets offered to railwaymen and their families. Though the Peak District farm always seemed cold and spartan compared with home, Ben was always pleased to see us and particularly enjoyed showing all his animals, from the sturdy horses to the new-born calves and lambs; because of this the two-day visit provided us with a welcome break in routine plus the excitement of a long train journey.

We all came face to face with Ben as we were fleeing down the platform chased by the angry junior porter.

'Whoa, beauties,' he said as though speaking to his farm horses, 'are you in such a hurry to help with my cases?' His lined and weather-beaten face wore its usual smile but something about it warned us of trouble. At least his unexpected intervention had saved us from Joe.

However, it did not save us from the strap, which was laid on each of us forcefully by Father when he heard of the trolley incident. Although the air soon cleared, the event still seemed to carry foreboding, which was somehow connected with the arrival of Uncle Ben. At first he acted in his usual kindly avuncular way. He told us stories and took us out into the countryside, where he fascinated us with his knowledge of animals, even the most humble like slugs and spiders. In return we showed him our discoveries, which would often surprise him, because on Purbeck there flourished plants and insects which he had never seen in Derbyshire.

When not with us he pottered about the station getting under people's feet, especially old Fred Thomson's; he looked after Sam, the old carthorse who shifted wagons about the goods yard. At this time we would often come across Mother and Father speaking quietly to each other. When they saw us they would exchange glances and fall silent. Day by day Ben's shoulders seemed to grow more and more hunched, and he also became less eager to accompany us on walks, preferring to wander off on his own. 'You'll have to be kind to Ben,' said Mother, 'he's fallen on bad times.'

'Well I hope he goes home soon,' I said, 'it's not fair having to share my bedroom with Sarah.'

My selfishness may have been sensed by Ben though I don't

believe that I showed him any coolness. If I did I am eternally sorry, for it may have been the last straw to him. One evening he did not return to tea. It was a brilliant September evening and we decided to walk up the line a bit, the boys taking a catapult to shoot at rabbits. At the second milepost the track enters a cutting and goes underneath a bridge. Close to this was a plate-layers' hut. Uncle Ben had chosen to launch himself into eternity from its roof. His body was still turning slowly on the rope when we first saw him: he had tied the noose to the branch of an overhanging oak tree.

I have never been able to cleanse this terrible vision from my memory, and that awful moment when we realised that the object swinging on the end of the rope was Uncle Ben is still real.

As the eldest child it was I who had to give evidence at the inquest. Our parents blamed themselves for Ben's death, for not recognising his withdrawal into despair. It was at this time, however, that Mother became a friend as well as a mother. She explained Ben's desolation at losing the things he loved – his farm and animals – and how he had come to us, the only relatives he could turn to, to find sanctuary, but we had not succeeded in giving him the consolation he was seeking. (Although she reproached herself with this she was also angry with him. 'Why couldn't he have thrown himself off Dancing Ledge like most do?' she said. 'They're no trouble to anyone.')

It was a sign of our new relationship that she allowed me to be with her when she went through Ben's things, a task Father refused to do. It was, of course, a sad affair. We discovered a bundle of letters tied with ribbon – relics of an affair with a neighbouring farmer's wife, which surprised my mother. He was not penniless: the livestock had raised a few hundred pounds which were kept as sovereigns wrapped in an old sock. The last discovery was the most unsettling – a skull polished yellow with age, whose unseeing eyes gazed up at us from an old shoe-box.

'You can throw that out for a start,' said Mother when she saw it, and continued sorting his clothes – mainly into sacks for the rag-and-bone man. I picked up the skull from its nest of tissue paper. It was the first human remain I had ever touched, and I was fascinated and repelled at the same time.

'Why did he keep this?' I asked, wondering if it was a custom with lots of grown-ups to keep similar reminders of mortality. 'Who do you think it is, or was?' I added.

'How on earth should I know?' Mother replied impatiently. 'He was a funny old man in lots of ways. You'd best ask your father. Now put that in the rubbish sack and get on with it.'

I did as she said, though I placed it carefully so that I could rescue it later. I knew how much my brothers would like it.

We dug it out from the sack later. It was still in the shoe-box and looked even more sinister in the dusky light of the kitchen yard. Footsteps could suddenly be heard approaching the back door. Without a word I picked up the shoe-box and took it into the outside privy, bolting the door behind me. I heard the other children scampering away as my father approached. I looked round in the dim light for somewhere to hide the box. There was a shelf with various oddments, but the shoe-box would be too conspicuous there. Standing on the seat I carefully placed it on top of the cistern, pushing it well to the back.

Other excitements took our minds away from the skull – there was the fire in the goods shed, followed by the collapse of a culvert at Langton which derailed the early-morning train and meant that the line was closed for a couple of days. The great October gale drove a coaster onto the shore below Ballard Point and we were able to watch the rescue from the clifftop. The gale was also blamed for the worst accident at this time, when Stanley, a fireman from Wareham who was a great favourite with us, was blown from the front of his loco. He was trying to get the smokebox door open when a gust caught it and sent him off the buffer-beam and into the path of a wagon that was being shunted. He died instantly.

Although we children recognised these disasters and the anxiety that they were causing Father, we were preoccupied with the health of Sam, the railway horse. Since the death of Uncle Ben his behaviour had become very strange and Fred Thomson said he believed he was pining for the old fellow Where before he had been a keen and willing worker hauling the heavy wagons to their appointed positions in coalyard or goods shed, his nature was now awkward and stubborn and his performance lacklustre.

'He'll have to go,' said Father to Fred one day when Sam had ignored Fred's shout and sent a coal-wagon smashing into a van that men were unloading. Fortunately no one was hurt, but it was a near thing.

'Give him a last chance, sir,' pleaded Fred, 'he'll get over it.' The matter was left with Sam on probation.

Sam sealed his own fate, however, the following week. When Fred came to his stable to prepare him for the day's work Sam turned nasty and aimed a vicious kick at his groom. Fred managed to dodge this but was pinned to the wall by the horse, who just leaned on him, slowly squeezing the life out of him. With almost his last breath Fred managed to attract the attention of a passing permanent-way man, who pulled Sam off. Fred told how he was completely unnerved by the malignant gaze the horse turned on him as he fought for breath. He didn't object when the knacker was called.

'It almost seems like there's a curse on the place since Ben died,' remarked Father that evening. It was this comment which sparked thoughts of the skull in my mind. I went outside to see if it was still in its hiding-place.

If it had looked sinister by daylight, by lamplight it looked

A Class 3 tank engine on a branch-line working in 1952

positively evil. I hated it but picked it up out of the shoe-box, wondering how to dispose of it, when I saw that there was more paper below the layer of tissue on which it rested. I took out an old exercise book which was untitled but whose pages were filled with Uncle Ben's careful handwriting. I put the skull back and took myself off to bed early with the exercise book, whose pages were grubby and frayed with use.

I Found that it had started life as Ben's farm account book. The figures showed the relentless decline in his fortune, and he had given up entering them about ten years before. After this came the fascinating story of the skull, written partly in his own words but mainly in those of others, copied out in his painstaking hand, probably from library books. It concerned a skull which over the centuries had acquired a name – Dickey – as well as a reputation for supernatural power. Ben had arranged his thesis with scholarly care. It began:

'The earliest record of Dickey dates from 1807 and comes from Hutchinson's Tour of the Peak:

There are 3 parts of a human skull in the house and which I traced to have remained on the premises for nearly 2 generations past, during all the Revolutions of owners and tenants alike.

As to the truth of the supernatural appearance, it is not my design to either affirm or contradict, though I have been informed by a credited person, a Mr Adam Fox, who was brought up in this house, that he has not only heard singular noises, and observed singular circumstances, but can provide 50 persons within the Parish who have seen an apparition at this place.

He has often found doors opening to his hand...the servants have been repeatedly called up in the morn.

Many good offices have been done by the apparition at different times, and in fact, it is looked on more as a Guardian Spirit than a terror to the family, never disturbing them, but in the case of approaching death of a relative or neighbour, and showing its resentment only when spoken of with disrespect, or when its awful memorial of mortality is removed. For twice within memory of man, the skull has been taken from the premises...once on building the present house

17

on the site of the old one, and another time when it was buried in Chapel Churchyard.

But there was no peace! No rest! It must *be replaced.*

After reading this I began to realise that my intuition about the skull was correct. But how had Uncle Ben come to have it in his possession? I hoped that I might learn more from the following pages.

Apparently the most famous legend attached to the origins of the skull was that it had been that of Ned Dickson, a yeoman farmer who had left his land to fight for King Henry IV in France. His bravery saved his lord, Earl Willoughby, from capture at Navarre, but at the end of the battle he was struck down and gravely injured. The legend was told in the verses of a Victorian ballad:

And his life was preserved: but his strength was all gone
He rode not, he walked not, he stood not alone:
His battles were finished, his glory was o'er:
All ended war's pageant, he must see it no more.

Somehow the wounded warrior managed to return to his farm at Tunstead near Chapel-en-le-Frith. By this time his heirs (a cousin and his wife) had taken their inheritance, believing him dead. At first they could not believe that the wan figure on the doorstep was their relative but at last they seemed convinced and made him welcome, feeding him and putting him to bed in the best chamber. Once he was asleep, however, they crept back to the room and strangled him. But retribution followed:

But a year had not passed when one winterly night,
That the storm rack was hiding the moon from their sight,
Honest Jack and his helpmate cowered over the lum,
His visage was sad and her clacker was dumb.

'What's that i' the nook, John?' she suddenly cried,
And shaking with terror, they clearly espied
The head of Ned Dickson upright on the stone
As wan and as ghastly as when he was done.

Many years passed away and the murderers fell,
By just retribution as ancient folks tell:

By a blow from her husband the woman was killed,
By the fall of an oak Jack Johnson's blood spilled.

But the head of Ned Dickson still stood in the nook,
Though they tried to remove it by bell and by book;
Though wasted of skin, and of flesh, still the skull
Will remain at its post till its weird be at full.

One final quotation is relevant to what comes after. This concerns the building of the London and North Western Railway:

Everyone in the Combs valley [where Dickey lived] *believed that it was by Dickie's influence and objection to new-fangled ideas that the bridge being erected by the London and North Western Railway Company across the road passing near Dickey's residence was swallowed up in a quicksand. The Railway Company and Contractors battled against the malign influence for a long time but were eventually compelled to give way, and not only to remove the bridge to some distance, but form a new highway at a great expense for upwards of a quarter of a mile.*

From this it appeared to me that we were in even deeper trouble: not only did Dickey resent being taken away from his home but he also hated railways. No wonder we had suffered so many disasters! It seemed obvious that somehow we had to get the skull back to Derbyshire. I was wondering how we would be able to accomplish this when I came upon a loose piece of paper slipped between the last pages of the exercise book. It was in Uncle Ben's hand, but written more carelessly, almost scrawled:

I realise now how wrong it was to steal the skull. It did not restore the fortune of the farm, rather the opposite. May whoever reads this please replace it at Tunstead Farm. I pray that no further evil follows.

I was relieved at finding this; at least it was something that I could show to Father, though I still feared that he might dismiss it as superstitious twaddle. I was also afraid that my disobedience in not having disposed of the skull in the first place might make my mother angry. I was right about this, at

19

least, as initially she was furious, but when she read the exercise book she realised that worse disasters might have happened if we had simply sent the skull to the tip. At least we had a chance to end the spell.

My father was at first incredulous at the story – not so much with regard to what had happened at Swanage, but at Ben's stupidity in stealing the skull. Of course Father had been brought up with the legend, though he admitted that as a lad he had been inclined to scoff at it. He was soon making arrangements for a trip to Derbyshire and Dickey was restored to his traditional position (apparently Father left him in his shoe-box on the doorstep of the farm like an abandoned new-born baby). With Dickey gone Swanage became peaceful again, although few people would walk past the plate-layers' hut at night even though the railway had formerly served as a useful short-cut.

Many years later I was at a family funeral in Derbyshire and took the trouble to look up the history of Dickey at the library. I found that the owners of the farm at that time had recently told a local historian '...that no mystical demonstrations have taken place during their occupation, and they resent the many foolish misstatements and the vulgar curiosity which compels them to refuse to allow the skull to be seen'. Perhaps Dickey's trip to the seaside had finally laid his ghost.

The Swanage Branch was completed in 1885 after twenty-five years of political and legal struggle and two Acts of Parliament (1863 and 1881). The coming of the railway brought about vast changes, not only to Swanage, which soon grew from a fishing village into a Victorian holiday resort, but to all of the Purbeck area.

The line, operated by the London & South Western Railway, was immediately successful and played its part in peace and war until it was closed by British Rail in January 1972. Even before closure the Swanage Railway Society was set up to reopen it, though they were not allowed to undertake any work until 1976. Swanage station and much of the line were by then very dilapidated, but years of hard work and determination

A busy August day at Swanage with a train ready for departure to Harman's Cross

eventually succeeded in bringing back steam trains to Swanage.

Today Swanage station is immaculate and trains run for three-and-a-half miles to Harman's Cross. Moreover track is relaid to Corfe Castle and Norden, and the aim of linking up with British Rail at Wareham looks clearly attainable.

Retribution

Despite the weather it had been a good day for William Torry, the 'commercial gentleman' who sat alone in the freezing first-class carriage of the Whitby train. His day at Malton had been a convivial one, spent in the company of one of his most valued clients, Mr Branson the miller, to whom he had sold a fair number of the sacks which were his livelihood. The size of the order had been a pleasant surprise, and the bonus at lunchtime had been his introduction to an acquaintance of Mr Branson, a farmer who had promised to purchase two hundred of the best for his potato crop, which he was about to take out of clamps.

The lunch at the Green Man had been a very congenial occasion, an excellent steak pudding washed down with quantities of Tadcaster ale which, he thought uneasily, could prove a problem to his comfort on the journey back to Whitby. He rummaged beneath his overcoat for the fob-watch and by the dim light of the oil-lamp saw that the train was due to depart from Malton in less than a minute – not enough time for a last dash to the convenience at the far end of the platform.

To distract himself he opened the valise on the seat beside him. As he did so the carriage door opened and he was joined by another traveller, also well wrapped against the cold. After a moment he recognised the man who had shared his compartment earlier in the day – John Mickle, the representative of a furniture manufacturer.

'John! It's good to see you. I was fearful that you had caught the earlier train and left me to spend the time alone in the chill of this contraption.' As he spoke he continued to rummage in the valise, and he gave a grunt of satisfaction when he felt the silver flask and tumblers he was looking for. 'Here, have a measure of the best navy rum to warm the cockles.'

He handed a tumbler to his fellow-traveller, who took it wordlessly but gave a grateful nod. Abruptly the carriage door was opened and two foot-warmers were thrust inside.

'I thought we had been forgotten. It will be a bitter journey

NER station staff at Whitby – a photograph by F.M. Sutcliffe c.1890.

tonight even with these comforters. Already we are late in leaving: it's past eight now and we should have been off five minutes ago.' Torry was annoyed that there had been time enough for him to leave the train to relieve his bladder, but was distracted from this thought by the locomotive jerking the train from a standstill with an explosion of smoke and steam which set the wheels fighting for a grip on the wet rails.

'So how has your day been, John?' Torry asked against the clatter and creaking of the wooden four-wheeled carriage as the train gathered speed. 'Were you successful in your dealings with the wealthy widow?'

On the outward journey his companion had told him of his dealings with a woman whose husband had recently died. The latter had been a wool merchant in Bradford and his widow had chosen to build herself a new mansion near Malton, the town of her birth. John Mickle was the agent for the high-class furniture-maker and had received a valuable order for a vast sideboard and a dining table with chairs. Today's visit, not the first occasion of meeting her, had been to finalise the details of decoration.

His friendly enquiry met with a silence which Torry felt to be almost hostile, but then Mickle leaned forward from the seat opposite and began to speak with a rush of words.

'I saw you for the first time in my life this morning and felt then that you were a man who could be trusted. Please forgive me for burdening you with my misfortune, but my feelings are so inflamed that I must tell someone of the dilemma that fell upon me today.'

Inwardly Torry groaned at the likelihood of the rest of the journey being turned into a confessional. The cold and the jolting of the carriage were already making him feel most uncomfortable and he knew that it was at least another thirty minutes before the brief stop at Pickering would allow him a quick dash to the urinal. As a distraction he poured two more tots of rum and settled back to listen to his companion's woes.

In contrast to the earlier torrent of words Mickle's speech was now hesitant:

'When I told you of my business in Malton this morning I failed to mention the attachment which had grown up between myself and the widow. I found her a passionate and attractive woman not yet into middle age, who kept making excuses for me to call upon her, at first for business reasons, but later for more pleasurable purposes. Today she announced herself to be hopelessly in love with me and begged me never to leave her. This caused me consternation since, though I looked forward to the trysts, I regarded them merely as inter-ludes of mutual physical passion and little more. I am some years younger than she and have a family that I would be heartbroken to leave. There were tears and recriminations when I parted from the widow today, and as I climbed into the brougham she handed me this letter which she had obviously written before our meeting and which I was only able to read by the station light at Malton.'

He handed Torry an envelope which had been roughly opened: it still carried a slight hint of feminine fragrance about it. Torry fumbled in his vast pockets for a box of matches, took the letter from its envelope and struck a match, peering closely at the letter in order to read the handful of words scrawled across the sheet of pink notepaper.

*Darling Dodo, you know how I love you and suffer when I am
not with you. You have told me you will not leave Sarah and
the children, but if you do not take this course I will tell her
myself of all that has happened between us. I know that we
can be eternally happy together and that this is for the best.
With my everlasting love, your Adeline.*

The light from the match faded as Torry read the last words
of the note, and he turned his eyes towards John Mickle, who
was just visible in the meagre glow of the oil-lamp which was
the compartment's sole illumination.

'It's certainly a sad pickle you find yourself in, John. It is the
classic conundrum, a trap from which there is no easy escape.'
William Torry noticed thankfully that the train was slowing
on the approaches to Pickering. 'Will you please excuse me for
a moment here, as I have to make a call of nature and will
also try to obtain refreshment.'

He eased his burly figure through the door as soon as the
train was stationary and made towards the cloakroom. A few
moments later he was at the refreshment trolley on the platform, almost opposite the carriage where the silhouette of
John Mickle could be seen through the window. Torry returned
to him bearing two sausage rolls and a small bottle of rum to
replenish his flask.

'It never ceases to amaze me how the North Eastern
manages to capture the essential flavour of its railway in the
food it supplies,' he remarked genially as he took a bite from a
sausage roll. His companion had refused the one he had been
offered but had accepted another tumbler of rum. 'Here', Torry
continued, 'I can distinctly taste coal, oil, fish and sweat.'

The train whistled and began to pull away from Pickering;
Levisham would be the next stop some six miles distant.
Large flakes of snow drifted past the windows of the carriage.
Soothed by the food and the rum and with his earlier discom-
fort now eased, Torry felt drowsy and disinclined to continue
the conversation. He reflected that Mickle's situation was
hardly unique and that throughout the course of history men
had found themselves in the same dilemma. Few loving wives
would ignore or forgive a husband's peccadillos, and a lifetime
of coldness seemed a bitter price to pay for a few brief, albeit
passionate, encounters.

'The Climb to Goathland'

'Had I taken up the widow's offer I would have become a laughing-stock, a contemptible plaything ridiculed by society and treated with disdain by the servants. Neither would I have had a business to conduct, for who would respect a man living in sin with an older woman on whom he had to rely for financial support?'

Mickle spoke these words almost to himself and Torry took little interest in them as the train rocked and swayed towards Levisham. The driver and his fireman on the footplate at least had a fire to keep their fronts warm, though the open cab gave little enough protection against the large wet snowflakes which were now swirling from the sky. Again the sounds coming from the wheels changed as the brakes were applied, and the train slowed as it approached the station at Levisham.

'Would she truly have done this to one she loved?' Mickle's words, which Torry took to be self-pitying, were almost lost in the bustle of their arrival. A porter swung his lantern as he walked along the train calling out the name of the station. A handful of people had alighted from the second- and third-class carriages and put their heads down as they walked into the blizzard. Doors slammed, the locomotive snorted, and then it jerked its train into life again. The most arduous part of the journey was about to begin for the engine-crew, and the stoker piled shovelfuls of coal through the firebox door as fast as he could. In the next two miles the train would climb one of the steepest stretches of line to be found on the railways of Britain, as the track surmounted gradients as steep as 1 in 50 in Newton and North Dales on the way to the moorland summit at Fen Bogs. As the name suggests this swampy patch of ground had been a difficult obstacle to the builders of the line, who eventually overcame it by putting down foundations of hurdles covered with brushwood and heather before laying the ballast and track on top. With the summit reached, the train began to move more quickly. The change of pace woke Torry from a doze and he again refilled the tumblers.

'Since you have been so confiding about your circumstances let me distract you from your problems for a moment by telling you of contrasting ones which once befell myself.'

Mickle gave no sign of hearing these words, but undiscouraged Torry continued:

'This is a story from my history which I trust you will never reveal to a soul; I have never told it before but you should take it as the truth.

'I was once in the employ of a wealthy manufacturer who was an ogre, a man as cruel as he was mean. He beat and starved his apprentices, showering them with incessant scorn and abuse as well as occasional storms of blows. He cheated us of our rightful wages and by keeping us impoverished and indebted bound us to him in a kind of vicious circle. If any had the temerity to attempt to leave him he would take poisoned words to the new employer and the man would soon be out on the street. It was nothing less than slavery to work for such a man in a town as small as ours.

'Evil begets evil and one night he drove us too far: it was a tempestuous night of wind and flood, and when in a moment of outrage the burliest of my workmates laid him flat with a poker it was but the work of a moment to tip him into the harbour which lay just across the road. There the tide, swollen by torrents from these moors, quickly took him out to the German Sea. Although rumours abounded for a few weeks no proof could be found to explain his disappearance and, since we had only helped ourselves to a part of his concealed hoard of riches (believing that it was owed to us) the whole affair was soon forgotten. Most of us were not long in finding more worthwhile and profitable pursuits. For myself, I bought a share of a sacking business from which I enjoy a modest profit. I have never allowed the incident to disturb my conscience.'

The concluding words were delivered in an almost smug tone just as the train slowed in approaching the top of the

Goathland incline. Because the descent from the moor was so steep the carriages had to be lowered at this point by means of a ropeway.

Torry reached into another of the capacious pockets of his heavy coat and drew forth a cigar-case which he offered to Mickle. The latter selected a cigar and bit off its end as Torry lit a match. It was as Torry leaned close to Mickle with the light that he saw his shirt and cravat for the first time. Both were soaked in blood, and some drops had spilled onto his waistcoat and even his velvet outer garment.

'By God, are you injured?' stammered Torry.

'No, I am perfectly all right,' replied Mickle calmly.

There was a moment of silence as Torry took in the implications of this remark.

'Then whose is the blood?' he asked, though his faltering tone betrayed dawning realisation.

'Of course it is the widow's. I had my moment of intolerable rage too, against the trap that I found myself in, and returned

'Up the Coast' – Sandsend, just to the north of Whitby

to kill her. I thought my scarf would have hidden the blood. You may turn me in when we reach Whitby; I do not care to go on with this. And by the by, your secret will be safe with me.'

At this moment the train gave a soft jerk forward as, with the rope attached, it was nudged towards the incline by the locomotive. Once on the slope it gathered pace quickly and they could hear the brakes of the incline van being applied. Bright sparks appeared outside the carriage windows as they took hold. Suddenly there was an almighty jolt as the slack of the rope was taken up but then, instead of slowing, the carriages were speeding onwards at an ever-increasing rate. The last image held in the minds of the two doomed men in the first-class carriage was a spectacular shower of sparks falling with the snowflakes, before with a resounding crash the brake-van left the rails and the wooden carriages ran into it, parts of them splintering like matchwood.

After the explosive crescendo of the crash, silence. Here and there light flared as pools of spilled lamp-oil were ignited. One of these illuminated a hand clutching a sheet of pink note-paper. As the flames stretched upwards the fingers of the hand relaxed and released the letter which, already burning, fell amongst the wreckage.

The railway between Whitby and Pickering started life as a horse-drawn line in 1836, steam locomotives taking the place of horses in 1847. Many of the railway's employees had formerly worked on stage-coaches, and the horse-drawn traffic was worked in a remarkably similar way, each carriage having a driver and postilion. The design of the carriages was an unashamed copy of the stage-coach and they were even given similar names. When steam locomotives took over from the horses most of the stage-coach men carried on working for the railway and Sedman, the guard aboard the train which crashed at Goathland on 10 February 1864, had previously filled a similar post on stage-coaches. He stayed in the brake-van after the rope broke on the incline, and for his subsequent bravery in rescuing the survivors was rewarded with a public subscription of sixty guineas.

The inquest into the accident concluded that it was caused by the rope breaking (it had been run over and was due to be

Incline Cottage at Goathland – the scene of the disaster

replaced the next day). Further, too much slack had been allowed on it at the top of the incline, and the system of braking caused the brake-van to derail (two iron shoes were lowered from the van directly onto the rails; the wheels themselves had no brakes).

Had the van not left the rails the carriages might have stayed on the track and survived intact, simply running away to a spot far beyond the bottom of the incline.

Thirteen people were injured in the accident and two killed – the two commercial travellers featured in the story. The incline at Goathland lasted until 1865, when the 'Deviation Line' was opened, taking a more circuitous route to reach the top of the moors.

The railway then continued to serve the North Yorkshire community for another hundred years, but in 1965 the Beeching axe closed the section between Malton and Grosmont leaving only the last six miles into Whitby, over which the Esk Valley line trains from Middlesbrough still operate.

Luckily, the historic line was not allowed to die and a group of enthusiasts set about restoring the eighteen miles south from Grosmont to Pickering through the heart of the North Yorkshire Moors, with only the six miles across the flat Vale of Pickering towards Malton remaining permanently closed. The enthusiasts repaired the track, reinstated the signalling, improved the stations and brought in locomotives and carriages, and in 1973 the Duchess of Kent formally reopened the Pickering to Grosmont line as the North Yorkshire Moors Railway.

Today the railway is busier than ever, with steam trains running every day from Easter to November. Then there are dining-car trains serving sumptuous meals at weekends, and Santa Claus makes regular trips along the railway to dispense his gifts in the weeks approaching Christmas. The growth in popularity has been so phenomenal that some of the most powerful steam locomotives are hard pressed to lift their heavy trains up the demanding gradients, to the wild moorland which makes this line scenically unique amongst Britain's preserved railways.

The Colonel and Old Shuck

The bald man with the pointed beard and blazing, fanatical eyes nodded to the Colonel and resumed taking notes from the heavy philosophical work propped before him as the old gentleman returned to his seat. Although getting on in years the Colonel retained his upright military bearing. He enjoyed working in the reading room of the British Museum. It lent respectability to his research into what he still regarded as a rather dubious topic.

He reached for the first of the four books freshly delivered to his place. *Canine Beasts in Mythology* was a work already known to him, but he needed it to check on a reference, and put it on one side for study later on. The second book was in German – its title could be translated roughly as *Hell Hounds of the Baltic Lands* – and as his German quickly proved unequal to academic prose he put this to one side too. The third book, hardly much more than a pamphlet, he opened more eagerly. It had been written by a local cleric some forty years previously and distributed privately, only a hundred copies or so having been printed. *Old Shuck*, the *Phantom Black Dog of the Eastern Counties* had been unknown to him until the previous week, when it was casually mentioned at a luncheon party by William Marriott, the young engineer of the Midland and Great Northern Railway who lived at Melton Constable and who had shown an informed interest in almost every topic of conversation that had arisen. The Colonel had found Marriott excellent company and been surprised to find himself agreeing to deliver a lecture on his new hobbyhorse – the Black Dog, a spectre that had terrorised the district for generations – at a meeting of the Mechanics' Institute at Melton in three weeks time.

'The men will welcome the relief from their usual diet of engineering wonders,' Marriott had said, 'and they may be able to add substance, if that is the appropriate word for a ghost, to your research.'

The Colonel turned the opening pages of the slender volume, reading the usual background to the mystery which extended back to the earliest written records. The Vikings knew legends of the Hell-hound whose glance, from fierce yellow eyes as big as saucers, brought certain death. A Yorkshire monk writing in the thirteenth century had listed a series of occurrences in which a stray black dog, as big as a donkey, had spread panic through the district. Closer to home, Old Shuck of Bungay was even more notorious having torn through the parish church as a violent thunderstorm raged overhead. As the beast ran between two local worthies who were at prayer, 'It wrung the necks of them bothe at one instant clene backward, in so much that even at a moment, where they kneeled, they strangely dyed.'

This was all well known to the Colonel and his fingers restlessly flicked the pages as he reached the end of the booklet. Suddenly he paused as he saw the reference which Marriott had mentioned:

An express hauled by a Johnson-designed 4-4-0 in full cry on the M & GN in the Edwardian era

...Close to a place named Sherringham in Norfolk a dog alarmed the neighbourhood for some weeks, this occurring about thirty years ago. Two infants were carried off by the beast and never seen again. Some common folk were in mortal fear and said that the animal was not of this world but a ghostly Hell-hound sent to swerve them from their evil lives. Others held that the children, who disappeared on separate occasions, had strayed too close to the work of smugglers.

It was obvious that the author was inclined to believe the latter suggestion. Though the information was meagre enough, the Colonel felt satisfaction at having traced it.

Having glanced at the remaining book, which proved to be of no interest at all, the Colonel rose from his chair and, having murmured 'Good day' to the bearded man, left the Reading Room to catch the afternoon Cromer Express from King's Cross which he knew would bring him to his Norfolk home in time for supper. He had chosen Sheringham (as it is spelled now) as the place to spend his final years after three decades in the service of the Queen. A tiny fishing village before the coming of the railway, it was now becoming a resort popular with like-minded gentry, and the Colonel occupied one of the first, and most imposing, of the mansions to be built on the clifftop.

The lecture at the Mechanics' Institute went well. The audience, nearly all of them men who worked on the Midland and Great Northern, were attentive and asked serious questions afterwards. There were none of the flippant comments that the Colonel had feared, and the reason for this soon became apparent. It was William Mobsby, a goods-train guard, who first hinted at the respect that the employees of the railway felt for Old Shuck:

'Sir, I wholly appreciate your bringing this affair into the open: it's something I myself and many of my mates have known about for years. In fact I have heard tell that Shuck plagued the men who put down the track, and there were some, proud and bold before, who left the work because of him.

'My experience is a little different from that suffered by many of us here tonight. I was on a pick-up goods and we hit a pheasant just before Weybourne. It was at first light on a chill

February morning and the driver had all the time in the world to stop the train so I could pick the bird up, knowing it would be a welcome treat to put in our pot that night with dumplings, what with six children growing up.

'I got down from the van and walked back along the track. The sun was just rising above the sea but as I stooped to get the pheasant I felt a chill on my neck, and then there was a "whoosh" as something dashed past me with the speed of the wind. All I saw of it was a great black shape, like a dog but four times bigger than any I ever did hear of. We thought at first it must have been some animal or other escaped from captivity, but the more we talked of it the more unlikely this seemed. When it ran off it made no noise but seemed to glide over the track, and then just faded, like they say, into thin air.'

The audience, whose attention had been utterly held by the speaker, shuffled feet and coughed into their handkerchiefs as he sat down. There was a pause before another man rose, an older figure, his face weathered and his frame shrunken and stooped from years of labouring. His accent was very different from Mobsby's broad Norfolk dialect. He was Irish and spoke in the soft tones of the far west:

'I am called Pigeon Ryan, your honour, and was with this railway from the very start. Work was scarce then, sir, and this was one of the last big enterprises. I came here from the Great Eastern and had to go out with the surveyor. We often had to move sharpish because there were folks hereabouts who didn't take to the notion of a railway coming to disturb their peace. We were forbidden to set foot on some land and the keeper would be told to guard it as tight as if we were after his pheasants. Some would even put down traps against us. Anyway the upshot of this was that we were usually about in the half-light if we were in the grounds of a difficult customer. We often brushed with Shuck but the worst time was the last. We were plotting the line through Runton and Mr Mackenzie the surveyor, a fine young Scotsman, was bent over his level and I was holding the post when this beast sprang at us from nowhere. Mr Mackenzie ducked down but instead of passing over him it seemed rather to go through him. We both took off through the woods and ran for ten minutes or so up the hill onto the heath. When we stopped there was no sign of the animal, neither was there when we went back to the place for the level. But there was a sort of a smell there, as though someone had lit a match. Mr Mackenzie told me then that he had looked back just as the thing sprang and had seen the yellow eyes, big as saucers. I never told him what I knew of this demon (we would call it a banshee at home), that if you looked into his eyes it was as good as a death warrant, but it sure enough did for him. A fine healthy young fellow he was up to then, but he soon began to waste away and was dead within the twelvemonth.'

The sombre end to this story left the audience disinclined to comment further, and the chairman, a passenger guard named Roberts, duly thanked the Colonel and closed the meeting. As they left he asked his own question: 'Tell me, Colonel, have you yourself ever seen this beast?'

The Colonel replied quickly: 'Indeed I have, sir. It will be a year to the day at the end of this month.'

The funeral saloon had been brought south from the Great Northern and was now coupled next to the tender as the 8 am out of Cromer Beach waited at the platform.

'Sad old do,' remarked the stationmaster to the train guard while the last trunks and hampers were loaded into the van.

This is not a funeral car but the New Royal Southampton Railway Carriage of the mid-nineteenth century

An M & GN express c.1920

Roberts, the guard, nodded vaguely. He remembered only too well his last encounter with the Colonel only a few days previously.

He had spent some time reflecting on the words that the old gentleman had spoken privately to him at the end of the meeting, and had come to the conclusion that it was his Christian duty to offer him help – even though it was hard to imagine that such a man needed much in the way of spiritual comforting.

The Colonel lived alone in his large house apart from a Scots housekeeper nearly as old as himself. He had never married, and had no close relatives or intimate friends to whom he could confide the strange threat which hung over him. His character was what in Norfolk is called 'close': in other words he kept his troubles to himself, and he had surprised himself by his ready response at the meeting to the question about his own encounter with the beast.

The evening after the lecture Roberts cycled up to the Colonel's home on the cliffs and, in some trepidation, knocked at the door.

'I am sorry to call upon you at such an hour without appointment, sir,' he said having been admitted to the house, 'but I thought I might be able to help you with more information on the subject of Black Shuck.'

At this the Colonel could hardly fail to show courtesy and Roberts was soon installed in front of a blazing fire in the library with a large Irish whiskey in his hand.

The Colonel wasted little time in conversational preliminaries: 'My words to you after my talk were unguarded and you must not believe that I am disturbed by what I think I saw.'

'I can believe that, sir. It is after all only a local superstition.'

'You can hardly have been attending to what I said the other night if that is what you think of it, Roberts,' replied the Colonel. 'I have shown that its origins go back practically to the beginning of history.'

As a devout church-goer Roberts's feelings on the subject were ambivalent. His duty was obviously to disparage the idea of Black Shuck but he was a native of the district, had heard tales of the black dog since childhood, and was too honest to disguise his true feelings.

'Colonel, I am torn as to what to tell you. I cannot honestly say that what you have seen is meaningless. I know too many people about here who have gazed at those baleful yellow eyes and died soon after. If I can help you in any way at all please have every confidence in me, for I will tell nothing of this to any living soul.'

The Colonel looked at him for a long moment before replying.

'I believe you in that, Roberts, and appreciate your kindness in coming here tonight, but no, I can add very little to what you know already, and if my fate has been decided by my meeting Black Shuck then so be it. I have had a good life and a long one and am quite content.' He paused; on resuming, his words were slower and more thoughtful. 'In fact there is a curiosity in me to see how he may achieve his object. I suppose in that respect, if the worst befell, you might be of assistance.'

He had been pacing about the room as he spoke but now sat down opposite the railwayman and looked at him again intently.

'How am I going to tell a sceptical world of my destiny? I have become quite involved with the Hell-hound and would hate to leave the final chapter unwritten. I will attempt to entrust this to your care and although I will not go out of my way to meet with Shuck in the next few days, I have no fear of him and intend to live normally. However, should I die there will be an envelope addressed to you on my person. In it will be a notebook which I will endeavour to use if I meet with an emergency.'

The arrangement having been agreed, Roberts took his departure soon afterwards and his life resumed its ordered way, always dictated by the railway timetable. When he returned from church on Sunday evening he found the village constable waiting.

'Mr Roberts, sir, I am afraid I have unhappy news. We have just retrieved the body of Colonel Breck from the foot of the cliffs. It seems there must have been some sort of accident and he was killed by the fall. We found this package in the pocket of his coat. It's addressed to you.'

As he handed the envelope to Roberts he showed that he expected his curiosity concerning its contents to be satisfied, but the guard took it and put it unopened into one of his pockets.

'Tell me, Constable, how did the accident happen and where? Did anyone witness it? How was he discovered?'

The policeman replied that an angler walking along the beach had found the body which, even though it had fallen from the top of the cliffs, appeared uninjured. It did not seem as though he had been set upon and his watch and purse were intact. No one had seen the incident.

'It was his habit to take a constitutional after lunch on Sundays,' continued the policeman, 'and usually he'd go through the park, then over the road and railway and back along the clifftop. He was found below the cliffs almost opposite the bridge over the line. It's my belief he must have suffered a seizure while standing on the edge of the cliff and was probably dead by the time he reached the bottom.'

Roberts knew the spot well. The Colonel had walked down a cart track towards the sea, crossing the railway about a quarter of a mile before the cliffs. He said: 'Have you looked for signs of a struggle on the cliffs or in the loke?'

The policeman replied almost scornfully. 'We have that, sir,

'Call again Tomorrow' – an evocative picture of a rural branch-line in East Anglia

it was the first thing we did. So if you've nothing to tell us', and here he looked meaningfully at the pocket containing the package, 'I'll be on my way.'

Roberts closed the door and, to escape his family, took himself into the parlour where he lit the lamp and opened the envelope. The notebook was written in the form of a diary covering the days which had passed since his meeting with the Colonel. Nothing eventful had happened in the days up to Sunday and these entries were brief and to the point. However, that for Sunday was very different. It began normally enough:

Walked through the Park and met with Mr Upcher who was about to go out for a drive. He told me that the Prince is about to visit Lord Hastings. That will bring a to-do! Climbed the hill above the Hall and sat surveying the prospect in much the same way as Repton, of blessed memory.

The next entry was in writing which contrasted starkly with the neat script which had gone before.

Suddenly there is a strange chill in the air and my heart has begun to beat faster. It is as though I am the quarry of some beast of prey. I feel like a stag who peers about the landscape and sniffs at the air, seeking evidence for a deadly presence which he feels but his senses will not confirm.

The final sentence was in an almost illegible scrawl.

I have fled as far as I can run and still it stalks me like a cat with a mouse – I fear I am done for, farewell.

Roberts climbed into his van as the whistle blew and the train began its journey. The Colonel's remains were on their way to his family's mausoleum in Scotland. Ten minutes later the engine was straining at its load as it pulled out of Sheringham. The guard looked intently out at the gloom of the December morning. He had spent a restless night wondering what to do, his conscience torn between his loyalty to the Colonel and his strict religious belief. He saw the men arriving to work on making the new greens of the golf course, and then the train passed beneath the bridge which the Colonel must have crossed just before his demise. Roberts flicked the notebook out of the window and it flew amongst the trees of a wood on the hillside between the line and the sea. He knew that the trees stood on Dead Man's Hill.

The North Norfolk Railway is part of the former Midland & Great Northern Joint Railway, which ran a meandering course over 120 miles from the Midlands to the Norfolk coast. Most of it was closed in 1959 and the survival of the five-and-a-half miles from Sheringham to Holt is a tribute to the hard work and perseverance of the restoration society. Passengers will enjoy the opportunity of travelling through some of Norfolk's most attractive scenery, and be taken back to the time when the line was busy with holiday traffic. Enthusiasts will be particularly interested in seeing (and hearing) how the locos tackle the steep gradients of the line.

Sheringham is an attractive little seaside town with two stations, the North Norfolk Railway occupying the original three-platform station while British Rail use a new single platform where trains leave for Cromer and Norwich. A museum, shop and various displays at the old station are designed to keep visitors occupied until the departure of their train.

Most services from Sheringham are hauled by steam, though in dry summers diesels may take over at Weybourne, the half-way point, for the steep climb to Kelling Heath and Holt where sparks could easily set fire to dry bracken and gorse. The most prized locomotive is the newly restored B12/3, a unique survivor of the class which used to haul many express trains on the LNER network. One of the five industrial tank locos owned by the society may also be on duty while the beautiful little J15 0-6-0 is taking a well-earned rest.

The North Norfolk Railway is preserved as a tribute to the M&GN, the independent and much-loved line that was vital to the development of Sheringham and Cromer.

The Secret Accident

After the usual greetings, Lieutenant Pete G. Forster had written home to his parents:

...It's real cute country too, just like fairyland here in Devonshire County. Everything's so green, except the soil and that's red. The people that I've met have all been friendly and the kids are all over us for gum, chocolate and badges, in that order. My billets are in a big old inn, called the Royal Castle on account of some queen staying there about three hundred years ago. And she haunts the place still. They say if you stay up till two in the morning you'll hear her arrive in a coach with horses, but if you set eyes on her then you're a dead 'un.

Another thing is that I've met another railroad buff here called Tom who's a lovely guy. He's a pointsman and lets me sit in his cabin and yarn. Every little two-bit town in these parts has its railroad, some so small they'd fit into our yard back home!

Tom Rivett told me that tears filled his eyes when he first read this letter many years after it had been written. He had found it deep down in the comfortable old armchair which he had in his signal box at Kingswear, on the opposite side of the River Dart to Dartmouth and the terminus of the town's branch-line. He had promised to tell me his very own ghost story and the letter, which he had drawn out of a tattered envelope, formed the prelude to the story.

I was befriended by Tom in much the same way as the young American had been many years before. He was a kindly old boy, with twinkling eyes, a ruddy complexion, and luxuriant mutton-chop whiskers. The only time he ever became unkind was on the subject of women – he was married to a scold who was jealous of the only real passion of his life, the Great Western Railway. His voice was deep with a resonant Devon burr which always seemed to be on the brink of a chuckle. Both his father and grandfather had been railwaymen, while Tom had received his watch for forty years' service in

Coronation Year – 1953, which was the year I got to know him. I was thirteen then and a fanatical train spotter. I came to Dartmouth with my parents on holiday but spent little time with them, preferring to explore the byways of the Great Western with a Rover Ticket.

Tom had nodded to me a couple of times from his box. Then one day as I waited at the end of the platform he invited me up there, waving a teapot. I soon found that his knowledge of railways was fantastic, though he was hopelessly biased in favour of everything GWR. I came from LNER territory and stoutly attempted to defend the company. It led to some good arguments – Churchward against Gresley, and so on. If you really wanted to get him going you would praise Bulleid and the Southern – that was a red rag to a bull all right!

By the end of the holiday I was spending as much time with him as I could, and he took me out fishing as well as arranging for me to ride on the footplate of a Prairie tank up to Newton Abbot. I so enjoyed myself that I plagued my parents into arranging a similar holiday the following year, and again spent most of the time with Tom.

The next year saw Tom's retirement and I feared that he would be lost without his job. I need not have worried – he was quite happy pottering about with his boat and his allotment, and visiting the pubs in the evening, hoping to meet a railwayman who could bring him up to date with the gossip.

In the succeeding years I married and started a family. I still managed to keep contact with the old man. He seemed to change very little over the years apart from becoming shorter and stouter: he still wore his ruddy complexion and tremendous whiskers.

It must have been about 1970, when I was around thirty and Tom past eighty, when he told me of his ghost. It was a brilliant June day and we were sitting on the riverfront watching holidaymakers and boats when he pulled out the ancient envelope from his pocket and handed it to me.

'Read that,' he said, 'I've a story to tell you that's been on my mind some time. I never spoke of it to anyone before but now I worry that I might be taking it to the grave with me. You can please yourself whether you believe it or not, but I can tell you that I did see this man's ghost, clear as day.'

This photograph captures the unhurried tempo of life in the days of the Great Western. A GWR branch-line train simmers gently at Newton Abbot

He paused, taking in the beauty of the scene, the crowds in summer clothes, the sunshine and the river traffic while I read the letter. As if on cue, the sound of a train's whistle came from the other side of the water. Tom began:

'I remember it being a sparkler of a day just like this when I first met young Pete, who wrote that letter (and whether he hid it or lost it in the box we'll never know). Any road, it was September '43 and things were getting real busy for us. At first there was a trickle of nobs from the navy and army coming to the town, then there were special trains coming and going. There got to be so many that the carriage sidings at Goodrington were filled up a lot of the time. It was all very hush-hush too, with things being built on the river hidden by screens of tarpaulins, and great loads being brought in on low-loaders.

'Pete was a lootenant (that's how they said it) who was dead keen on railways. Now not many of the Yanks went out of their way to speak to us, but almost as soon as he arrived Pete was poking about the station. He got wrong with me by saying that to him a Great Western Castle looked like a toy loco. However, he was soon coming to see me at odd times in the box, just like you used to.

'The best times were the winter evenings when we would sit and chat over the stove. He would often come in with a bottle of their whisky, which was very welcome in those days. Of course he wouldn't say what he and the others were doing in Dartmouth but he did let slip that he was with an army corps that specialised in setting up railways. I guessed that he would soon be doing that in France.

'He was always on about the ghost at the Royal Castle. He would stay up and wait for it sometimes because it's supposed to happen in the autumn. Like I said to him, that's a dangerous game if you do catch sight of it because it's a ghost that doesn't like being seen. He told me that one of his mates had seen her, and that may be right in view of what followed.

'As winter drew on Pete found it more difficult to get away to chat with me. I saw him at Christmas when he brought a great basket of chocolate and stuff we couldn't get then for love nor money. There were all sorts of stories going about the town at the time – of people being turned out of their farms and cottages at Slapton and Blackawton just before Christmas and so on. When I asked Pete whether his lot had anything to do with it he sort of looked shifty and stared down at the mug he was holding without saying anything.

'After that he seemed to completely vanish from the scene, as did most of the Yanks, though the trains were still bringing in lots of big-wigs and heavy equipment. I missed his company – he couldn't argue as well as you but he was a clever young chap, and I can see him still, sitting in the old chair just like you did later.

'In the spring we guessed that things were being got ready for the invasion. Of course we never told our thoughts to strangers – like they said, 'Loose lips sink ships'. It all came to some sort of climax in April. Train after train came west. We dealt mainly with naval ones but I heard that the main line was jammed with them too – they even shunted twelve-coach trains up to Ashburton, and that took some effort. There was all sorts of trouble when they met with another long train coming down the branch the other way, where the passing loops only take five or six coaches!

'At the end of April there was a great shindig. We were used to bangs and thumps from the Slapton direction, but now it

Cromwell tanks being entrained at Winchester

seemed as though all hell was let loose there. Then one night we saw great flashes in the other direction, way out to sea towards Lyme Bay. It looked like Guy Fawkes. It all went quiet for a month or so – at least it did as far as the war went, because that's when Pete's ghost first came to see me.

'The first time was in the box on a warm night. I had gone out on the steps for a breath of air and when I came back inside there he sat, large as life, in the old chair. He was smiling in his gentle sort of way and wearing battle-dress, which I had not seen him in before. But he didn't answer when I spoke. I asked him how he was doing, would he like a cuppa, but he just sat there gazing back at me. "Are you all right, boy?" I said, and went towards him. I thought he might have had a sort of fit or something, just sitting there and not saying a word, but as I got nearer he sort of faded away and I was left thinking I must have dreamt it.

'But when a similar thing happened on the following night I realised it was a ghost I was seeing right enough. I began to talk to him of the things he knew, thinking it would comfort him. Perhaps it did, because for a while he became more adventurous and I would find him keeping me company as I walked back to the station at night. He never appeared in daylight or when there was anyone else about, and I was beginning to wonder if he was with me for keeps, and whether I should tell the vicar about him, when I realised that he was not staying so long and his shape was gradually becoming less distinct.

'By this time the invasion had taken place and we were a lot less busy. Come wintertime and he seemed to be more of a faint shadow than a ghost. Then, with the New Year, there was nothing to show of his presence in the box with me except the *feeling* that he was there. I don't believe that he was unhappy, or happy either, and I'll never know why he chose to haunt me, though I suppose it's flattering in a funny way.

'When even the feeling of his presence went I was sorry, though I suppose I should have felt glad that he was now at peace. He had given me the address of his parents, so after a little I wrote to them and told them of our friendship and asked how he was getting on. The reply puzzled me. They wrote a sad little letter back saying how Pete had been killed on the Normandy beaches soon after landing. He had spoken well of me in his letters and they thanked me for looking after him, and said that they would look me up after the war when they came to Europe to find his grave.

'Now all this was very strange to me. D-Day had been at the beginning of June, more than a month after the first appearance of Pete's ghost, and you couldn't very well have the spook of a living person, could you?

'All this I have kept to myself. Mind, I have heard one or two strange things since. Chatting to a couple of fishermen after the war I learnt how lots of bodies in American uniforms had been found along the coast before the invasion started. The police had come down hard on anybody who had fished these out, holding them in police stations for more than a month and only letting them go after D-Day. Then it all began to make sense to me. Something dreadful had happened before D-Day and it's been hushed up ever since. I know there's plenty of folks in this town as feels the same.'

Tom's story, which had none of the melodrama of his usual tales, was the more convincing because of this. He never mentioned it again, and died peacefully at the age of eighty-five. I still visited Dartmouth occasionally, mainly for the pleasure of riding on the restored steam railway which brought back so many memories.

In 1984 these memories were stirred again as a strange story began to emerge from the district. Big things were being made of the fortieth anniversary of the Normandy Landings and a newspaperman came to Slapton to investigate rumours of an Anglo-American cover-up of a disaster which had occurred just before the invasion.

It emerged that the area around Slapton had been evacuated because it provided a replica of the beaches and hinterland of the invasion zone in Normandy: it was the perfect rehearsal ground. The final dress rehearsal before the invasion was called Operation Tiger. During this exercise a flotilla of landing-craft approaching Tor Bay encountered a hostile patrol of fast torpedo-boats. Several of the landing-craft were sunk and many more damaged. Some 249 American soldiers and sailors were killed, though not all of the bodies were ever recovered. The disaster was due chiefly to incompetence, since the landing-craft were allowed to sail without air or naval support. Wartime security meant that the casualties were officially added to those of the D-Day landings, and this later gave rise to stories of a cover-up. The bodies that were recovered were buried in a mass grave at Slapton, though long before 1984 the grave was opened and they were reinterred in other cemeteries. The few local residents who knew anything of all this were sworn to secrecy, and, indeed, they kept silent about the circumstances of the tragedy for forty years.

I took the trouble to find out the official fate of Lieutenant Forster soon after I read the account of the misfortune of Operation Tiger. He had belonged to 557th Quartermaster Railhead Company, either sixty-nine or seventy-three of whose men were lost in the disaster (literally perhaps, as it seems that to this day the exact numbers of casualties are unknown). Pete's body was never recovered, though it may be of some comfort to his loved ones that Operation Tiger was a valuable contribution to the success of the landings on Utah Beach. Only two hundred men of the division lost their lives in this operation, a mere twenty-five of these falling in the initial assault. These figures are remarkably low when compared with those of other invasion sites.

Remember the Lootenant, and Tom Rivett, if you visit the memorial to Operation Tiger that stands at Slapton beach.

The Great Western Railway was without doubt the best known and loved railway in Britain and possibly the world. The Paignton & Dartmouth Steam Railway reflects a part of its history, and moreover offers the public an opportunity to experience the excitement of steam-hauled transport and recapture the halcyon days of the GWR in a uniquely beautiful setting. It also serves as a vital transport link between Paignton and Dartmouth in the summer, when inadequate roads are choked with traffic.

Amongst the locomotives which operate the line are representatives of two of the most famous classes of Great Western express engines – 7827 Lydham Manor and 4920 Dumbleton Hall. The rolling-stock includes a carriage with observation windows which allows all-round views of the River Dart. The vista seen as the train emerges from Greenway Tunnel – the river backed by steep wooded hills – is unsurpassed anywhere in the country. A popular excursion for holidaymakers is to travel from Paignton to Kingswear by train and then return from Dartmouth to Totnes by river and to Paignton by bus – a wonderful day out!

The monument to those killed in the operation on the shore at Slapton Sands

The Spotter

'Right then, lovelies, let's see if we can get it together!'

The young assistant director shouted through a megaphone at the crowd loosely assembled in front of the camera and then returned quickly to his position by the camera dolly. At his words the scene came to life. A girl presented a clapper-board to the camera and at the same time people began to move purposefully about their business on the station platform. In the near distance an engine blew a single note on its whistle and began to draw slowly into the station. It did not approach with dramatic gusts of smoke or steam since it was being pushed from behind by the railway's diesel shunter. The director of the film knew from experience that a loco making lots of smoke may look good, but the haze lingers for the rest of the day in calm conditions and draws a foggy veil over re-takes or further use of the location.

The activity grew frantic as the train drew to a stop. Porters, who with admirable regard to authenticity were waiting at the spot where the first-class carriages would come to rest, leapt forward to open doors. They were all smartly dressed in uniforms of the Great Central Railway, as worn in the early years of the twentieth century.

People began to alight from the carriages. The first-class passengers were dressed in style, the ladies taking care to gather up their skirts as they stepped to the platform. The men, most of them with imposing displays of whiskers and beards, had left the train first in order to help their ladies down.

There was no such gallantry about the third-class passengers. Most of them had jumped to the platform before the train stopped, many carrying bags or curiously shaped parcels, and were jostling other passengers in their rush towards the stairs leading to the exit.

During all this the camera was tracking in towards a brilliantly dressed woman who had got off the train from the rearmost carriage and was now running down the platform looking ecstatically happy and waving vigorously. A tall man ran towards her from the camera and, placing his hands around her waist, swung her up into the air.

'Cut,' shouted the young assistant, Tristan, as he saw the gesture made by the director. 'Let's take coffee now. Back in thirty minutes please, folks!'

He did not enjoy the next twenty minutes as the director raged about the inept way the scene had been handled. Its shortcomings were mainly blamed on Tristan – he had been responsible for rehearsing the scene with the extras, who had been drawn from the ranks of the local amateurs. The director, respectfully called the Maestro to his face, but Al Capone behind his back (he was Italian but had spent his early years in Brooklyn), could be violent at times and Tristan was wary of him. He looked at the ground as the Maestro shouted:

'Every one of the goddam bums is acting their ass off! The men all look like pansies and the women are putting on airs and graces enough for Shakespeare or Grand Opera! Every one of them is a goddam scene-pincher. You could have seen that yesterday; now we've got to waste time shooting it again, damn your eyes.'

And so the action was repeated, Tristan having diluted the Maestro's comments before passing them on to the extras. Afterwards the director nodded to his assistant and scowled. Tristan took this to be the nearest he would ever get to approval, and they went on to shoot four less demanding scenes at the location – Loughborough Central station, which had once belonged to the Great Central Railway but was now meticulously cared for by a preservation trust.

The final scene of the day was a romantic close-up of the two leads. It was shot hurriedly, for the light was failing fast and this time the engine pulling a goods train on the other line left a pall of smoke about the station which effectively ruled out any more photography.

'That's wraps on it for tonight then, people. Thank you very much.'

At these words the scene was galvanised once more. Extras hurried off to improvised dressing-rooms while the stars made for their luxury motor-homes. For the first time the technicians abandoned their air of bored indifference and moved energetically to pack away lighting-gear and cameras.

The director made stately progress towards his car without acknowledging the presence of any underlings, though he had managed a smile for the principal screen-actors as he dismissed them for the day. Once cocooned in the solitary comfort of his Rolls he poured himself a tumbler of brandy and ordered the chauffeur to drive back to civilisation – in this instance his Park Lane hotel.

The Maestro's first task the next day was to view the rushes in a private cinema in Wardour Street. Predictably it was *his* keen and practised eye which first drew attention to the fatal flaw in them.

'Who's that goddam kid?' he yelled as they watched the passengers disembark from the train. Remarkably, only a few of the viewers could see the figure who was upsetting him. In the opening scene a young boy lurked unobtrusively about the doorway of the refreshment room. This would hardly have mattered had he been dressed in clothes of the film's period – a sailor-suit or knickerbockers, perhaps – but he was clearly an anachronism. Wearing grey shorts, striped blazer, and fair-isle pullover, he was a child of a much later era.

'He's Just William,' said the Production Secretary, a formidable lady in her late fifties who remembered her childhood love for Richmal Crompton's rascally hero. Her comment meant nothing to the director, but the name was adopted by the others as the boy's presence was spotted in later scenes.

In the second take of the crowd scene (the train's arrival) 'William' had moved closer to the camera and could be seen more distinctly (though strangely there were still some present who swore they were unable to spot him). He gazed

A3 60111 (Enterprise) *in fine form with The Master Cutler*

intently at the proceedings, clutching a notebook and pencil. In the final scene, when the goods train steamed past, he made an entry in the book, perhaps the number of the engine, and chased off down the platform, presumably hoping for a closer look at it.

The Maestro looked round for someone to blame for the boy's intrusion. Tristan cringed, knowing that his last moments in the movie industry were probably at hand. Fortunately for him the director's wrath was diverted to the projectionist, who, as he emerged to ask whether they were finished with the viewing theatre, as he'd like to grab breakfast before the arrival of the next client, unfortunately chose to add a joking comment. He was sacked on the spot, though he didn't much care as he wasn't on the film company's payroll anyway.

William's intrusion spelt disaster for the Maestro, who was already 20% over budget on the production. He was sunk into a fathomless gloom as he ordered the previous day's shooting to be repeated.

Merchant Navy Class 35005 (Canadian Pacific) leaving Loughborough

William Benson's Friday-night chore was to collect the family's fish-and-chip supper from the chippie close to Central Station. He still clutched the order (with the ten-bob note rolled up in it) as he waited on the station platform. He knew that he'd be in trouble when he got home late with the supper but reckoned it would be worth it if something special was drawing the *Master Cutler* that night. He loved the excitement of the express's passage through the station. It went by at about fifty miles an hour, an explosion of sound and colour, which if you were standing on the platform made the ground shake beneath your feet. He jammed his cap tighter on the back of his head and buttoned his blazer as he heard the train whistle in the distance. It was a sound he did not immediately identify, different from that of locos he was used to, and he instinctively felt elated: this was going to be a good one, perhaps a 'namer' that no one else at school had bagged.

The ground began to vibrate as the express drew closer. It wouldn't be easy to spot the number with dusk drawing on so fast. Then the train roared by: the loco *was* something special, he realised in the last seconds left to him. It was an A3 Pacific – that much he was to know, but not its name, for as the great engine swerved over the points at speed the fire-irons which had been carelessly stowed by the fireman flew off the tender and hit the middle of the boy's body.

His death was instantaneous, though no one knew of the accident until passengers arrived for the next local about half an hour later.

His ghost began to be seen about the station soon afterwards. Few people minded very much since most of them knew who he was and that he was harmless. He was usually there when something momentous happened – the day the first 'Britannia' came through, the last day of British Railways' running of the line, and the opening day of the revived Great Central. You were more likely to spot him in photographs than *in situ*, but if you knew where to look you would see a tousled, becapped head hastily withdrawn into a doorway, or a small figure silhouetted at the end of the platform in the dusk.

Needless to say the film company had to abandon the location after even the most rigorous security failed to keep

William off the set. Look carefully when you next view something you know has been filmed at Loughborough – you may have the psychic gifts necessary to spot the Spotter.

The Great Central Railway's main line between Marylebone and Sheffield was opened in 1899 and was the last to be built in Britain. The route was constructed to the highest engineering standards of the day, and to the larger European loading gauge, to allow for use by continental trains which might come to England through the Channel Tunnel, then being surveyed. In its heyday the Great Central carried many expresses, the most prestigious being The Master Cutler. *After nationalisation the line was run at first by Eastern and then by Midland Region. The line was slowly run down and the last trains operated in 1969.*

After this a small group of enthusiasts set about the business of preserving a short section of the railway. Loughborough was chosen as the headquarters of the project and in 1974 a service started between Loughborough and Quorn. The line was steadily extended until in 1991 it reached the northern outskirts of Leicester, where the terminus occupies the site of the former Belgrave & Birstall station. It is also hoped that one day there will be further extension northwards to take the line to Nottingham.

Today there are about twenty steam locos and several diesels to operate the services, which include luxury dining-trains in addition to the comprehensive summer and weekend timetable. Enthusiasts will enjoy seeing the rolling-stock preserved here, which includes a seventy-five-ton steam crane and a travelling post-office train. The Great Central is also one of the few preserved lines running freight trains.

The railway is owned by shareholders and operated almost entirely by volunteers of the support group, the Main Line Steam Trust.

Trouble with Alice

The regular, slow-paced rhythm of wheels on rails seems to me to be a natural aid to thought. It is surprising that in the hundred or so years between the genesis of the railways in Britain and the start of their decline after nationalisation the abundance of spare time on duty allowed to three generations of railwaymen did not spawn even one great writer (although he spent much time on trains, Trollope was an employee of the Post Office). Signalmen spending hours alone in remote boxes amidst romantic countryside would, one might think, have been constantly inspired to put pen to paper. They could have painted, or written songs or verse. But no, over those hundred years little appeared that was memorable.

I am penning these words as I undertake the onerous duty of train guard on the Santa Special of the Buckinghamshire Railway Centre. I am very comfortably installed in a fine teak Gresley brake-van, and as the train (which is being hauled by our splendid 0-4-4 ex-Metropolitan tank) shunts slowly up and down the mile or so of track my duties are light enough to allow plenty of time for reflection.

Let me introduce myself. My name is Wainwright and I am a widower, an ex-schoolmaster sixty-seven years of age. I have made voluntary work here at Quainton a rewarding part of my hobby, which is the study of this country's railway history. My head is stuffed full to bursting with details of the rise and fall of the railway companies in the last century, and odd corners of my brain seem to hold on to an endless amount of trivia on the subject, loaded away there since boyhood when I was an avid reader of journals like the *Meccano Magazine* and *Trains Illustrated*. A few years before my retirement I fared reasonably well on *Mastermind* answering questions on (horrid word) 'railwayana', before coming unstuck on a statistical question in the semi-final. Forgive me, I now have to pause for a moment as we come to the end of another trip and have to load and unload another bevy of children.

I wonder whether 'bevy' was quite the right word in this context. Looking at the group which has just boarded the train

I think that 'regiment' might be the better word. Male tots of four or five have just been marched down the platform, an outing from a successful prep school of the neighbourhood. Wearing brand-new grey duffle coats (no hand-downs from older brothers here) they look like teddy bears. They are the designer-children of the prosperous stockbrokers and television personalities of the district – people who can afford the astronomic fees. It is sad that these days we receive far fewer field-trips from the state schools. I am afraid that enthusiasm for steam may die with my generation, the last to have known live steam on our railways. It is becoming much harder these days to recruit young folk into societies like this one. It is very difficult to capture the romance of steam railway travel even in a place like this, where we preserve some of the finest relics of the era.

But this is a hobbyhorse and I must not digress, even though it is one of the most interesting of these relics which lies at the heart of my story.

Last year I was one of the Santas. My reasons for not undertaking the task this year will soon become clear. We had a

'Dusk at Dore' – an LNWR scene close to Sheffield

different arrangement then: Santa did not visit each compartment of the train to dispense presents as is happening at this moment. Instead we made him a special retreat (I refrain from the word 'grotto') at the southern end of the line. There the children disembarked from the train, carriage by carriage, and filed in to see me one by one, returning to the train with their presents. I sat enthroned in my sanctuary, dimly lit by fairy-lights so that the cotton-wool beard did not appear too unconvincing. Each child was expected to whisper in my ear his or her ambitions regarding Christmas presents, and would then be sent away with a few kindly words about getting to bed early on Christmas Eve and not waking before dawn to open the gifts in their stockings. They would also be given a token gift appropriate to their age and sex.

In order to provide suitable accommodation for Santa we had moved one of our most prized exhibits up the line. This was the London and North Western six-wheeled picnic-car, which was intact though very fragile.

A word here about this vehicle which is, I believe, a unique survival. In the days when it was built it was possible to purchase such a carriage for your family and pay for it to be hitched to scheduled services. It would, for example, be joined with a Scottish express when the family wished to migrate to their hunting-lodge for grouse or stag shooting. It could also be used for attending race-meetings, or for picnic visits to famous beauty spots. Our example is even more unusual for having at one end an observation window made of curved glass. I believe that this was the first time glass made in this fashion was used in rolling-stock.

It must have made a splendid caravan. The family occupied a large and comfortable compartment while their servants, luggage and dogs were crammed into an adjoining one. They would be dropped off at a destination of their choice having travelled with all home comforts.

I must make another pause here while we replenish Santa's sack and install another train-load of youngsters more interested, I am afraid, in what gifts they will receive than in the joys and science of steam traction.

I am pleased to be able to report a better mix of youngsters this time. Santa Specials are particularly popular with grandparents who, I suspect, take on the children for a day while the parents go Christmas shopping.

Our initial restoration of the picnic-car made it weather-proof and it was first used as a convenient store, a place where our lady helpers stored jumble and other odds and ends. It was at this time that a whisper was heard of there being something a little odd about it. One of our ladies, a sensible woman married to an accountant who would have enjoyed his life much more had he been allowed to join the LNER at sixteen as he had wished, complained that, in the words of Stella Gibbons, 'there was something nasty in the woodshed', or in this case railway carriage. She could not be specific about what it was that she found upsetting, except that she refused to be left alone there again.

Most of us, I am afraid, took this rather lightly and teased her about it one day at coffee after a committee meeting. Unfortunately this embarrassed her and the incident marked the end of her work for the society. Yet it was hard to dismiss the incident entirely because it emerged that there had been rumours of things unpleasant before. The carriage had been discovered rotting in woods about ten miles from the Railway Centre. Its unique character was confirmed by an expert and the carriage bought from the landowner for a negligible sum. It cost much more to bring it back to Quainton, and it had to be dismantled first. During this operation an incident occurred which can only be interpreted in relation to later events. Two of our most reliable enthusiasts were working on the carriage in the gloom of a late-November Sunday after-noon. They were alone in the wood when, they said, they became aware of being watched. A short distance away, just beyond a patch of nettles, a young girl stood watching them solemnly. They described her as looking just like Alice in Wonderland. When they called to her she took no notice, and they had to return their attention to removing the roof since this operation was at a critical stage. She had gone when they were able to look again. They told the story to a handful of their friends that evening in the pub and, as usual in such cases, were told that they must have had too many pints at lunchtime.

My first meeting with Alice took place soon after I began my

LNWR guard, 1852

stint as Santa this time last year. I had taken the afternoon shift that day, the Monday of Christmas week. I walked down the line alone, donned my costume in the carriage, and settled back on my throne to await the train, my three sacks of presents around me. I swear that even then all was not normal. Of course there was always a chill about the place; it was only natural since we were unwilling to heat it, feeling that a portable gas or oil heater would detract from its ambience. But this time there was a *heavier* sort of cold, one you felt you could almost reach out and touch. It certainly felt warmer outside the carriage and was more cheerful, too, so I waited there until regular puffs of smoke and a toot of the whistle indicated that the train had started. I went back inside and was soon busy handing out presents and advice. More than ever I was amazed at the expectations of the young. Many already knew the gifts they would be receiving at Christmas – some costing many hundreds of pounds. Giving trial-bikes to five-year-olds is an astonishing idea to my old-fashioned way of thinking. The best present I ever had as a child was the fountain-pen I am using to write these words, more than fifty years on.

The last of the youngsters toddled back to the train with my usual words in his ears:

'Now you know that you mustn't open your stocking until daylight, otherwise Santa will hear of it and may leave you off his list next year.'

The train chuffed off back along the track and I was left alone with my thoughts. It was then that I noticed the girl watching me. In the dim light I could just see that she was pretty although wearing a very earnest expression. She stood looking at me through wide, deeply shadowed eyes. It was her clothes that set her apart from the other children I had seen that day. For a start she wore a hat, a beribboned straw boater. Her dress had flounces and though of fashionable length it was given an antique flavour by the lacy apron that she wore with it. My colleagues' description of the figure they had seen in the wood, as looking like Alice in Wonderland, came to my mind. It was indeed accurate: she looked just like Alice as drawn by Tenniel. I wondered about the wisdom of addressing a being that might well be a ghost, dimly remembering that you were meant to wait for the spectre to do the talking, but reflected that it hardly mattered what befell me at my time of life and so greeted her quietly:

'Hallo, have you come to see me?'

She continued to gaze at me steadily without moving. Then, as I watched, her outline seemed to dissolve into the gloom and I was left alone, reflecting on how many times in the past I had scoffed at the idea of ghosts.

After the next influx of children (for whom I had to make a determined effort to be the avuncular Santa they expected) I settled down hopefully to await the reappearance of my unearthly visitor. As the sound of the tank engine faded she returned, her image seeming to form itself from elements of the darkness. But this time she had not come alone: she held the hand of a small boy dressed in a sailor-suit. I estimated his age to be about four – Alice would be nine or ten. The boy was equally solemn. This time I feared to speak, but instead proffered one of the toys which I had unwrapped in readiness. However, neither child's eyes left my face, and as I gazed at them they both faded away just as Alice had done before.

I saw the pair once more, following the final train of the day. Normally I would have climbed surreptitiously into the guard's van, having quickly shed the Santa costume, and been given a lift back to base, but this time I made an excuse to the guard and lingered in the carriage. After about twenty minutes the two figures reappeared. Again I proffered a toy, an especially appealing teddy bear. This time I thought I detected a momentary shift of their eyes away from my face in the direction of the toy. When Alice looked at me again I saw that tears were flowing from her eyes. Deeply moved, I felt an irresistible urge to comfort her, and moved off my seat towards her. This movement broke the spell and the two children vanished abruptly.

This was my last sighting of Alice and her companion. The slow tears on Alice's pale cheeks will stay with me forever. Why should the children linger in such a strange existence, in neither one world nor the other? What were their motives in appearing to me? It struck me that the only way to bring peace to their restless souls was to find out as much as possible about their earthly existence – and the ending of it.

Santa stopping his train near Quainton

But where to begin? The obvious place was a library, and the most helpful was likely to be that of the National Railway Museum at York. There I found the complete records of the Wolverton Carriage Works, where I thought it likely that the picnic-car had been built. Unfortunately at this time I did not know the original number of the carriage, and there was no account of a special order having been fitted out with the distinctive windows of curved glass. However, there were one or two intriguing blanks in the records, which suggested to me that the patrons may have been Victorian celebrities who used their private carriages as mobile love-nests.

It then struck me that perhaps more productive research could be carried out closer to home. First of all I went to the gloomy spot in the woods where the carriage had last rested. There was little help to be found in this place, where nevertheless a strong feeling of unease persisted. I was glad to leave it, and made for the village close by and its two pubs (the usual source of information in rural communities). I drew a blank in the first, the picturesque White Lion, which had attempted to go up-market by introducing carpets, fancy food and loud music as well as about twenty brands of lager.

The other inn, the Fighting Cocks, existed in a time-warp. It was a proper village pub where it was still possible to find intelligent conversation and good beer. The helpful landlord, when he heard of my interest in the old carriage which had once occupied the woods, introduced me to Percy, a retired gamekeeper from the estate.

Percy knew the carriage well. Over his third free pint he launched into the story of the picnic-coach.

It had belonged to the Hannahs, a respected local family who had in past times enjoyed considerable wealth. They had once occupied the large house which overlooked the wood from a hill about half a mile distant. Their money had come from merchant banking, but the family suffered badly when its heirs were killed in the Great War and its fortunes dispersed amongst lesser relatives. An eccentric female Hannah, an unsuccessful artist, had converted the carriage into a dwelling just before the Second World War and had lived there until the 1960s, when she died in somewhat mysterious circumstances. On one of the coldest of winter nights she had taken herself off to wander in the woods dressed only in her night-clothes. Admittedly she was well on the way to being an alcoholic by then, but the inquest had been told that she was sober when she died 'of a massive seizure' as Percy put it.

He told me that she had always been a very strange woman, always restless and twitchy. She had never been able to keep a dog in the place – they either ran away or became morose and died. He had once tried to raise young pheasants in the wood but it was a gloomy old spot and he didn't much like spending time there, so only did it for the one season. This seemed to be the end of the story as far as he was concerned, but as an afterthought he said that there was someone in the village who might help, an old biddy named Peggy Roach who lived in the sheltered housing up by the church.

Peggy Roach proved to be a lovely old lady who, after initial uncertainty, enjoyed telling me about the reclusive artist, Sybil Hannah. She often dropped in at the old coach for a cup of tea, for she sensed from the first that the artist was lonely even though she appeared to discourage visitors.

'Of course Miss Hannah was a lot older than me and a whole lot posher, but she never put me down, and she loved the animals and flowers in the wood. She would lean her back against the trees and talk to them, said they needed encouragement. I reckon that her painting was a bit better than people thought, too. She gave me two or three of her pictures before she died, if you want to see.'

Up to this point I had explained that my interest lay chiefly in the origins of the old carriage and not particularly in the person who had inhabited it, but none the less I eagerly accepted the opportunity.

It was hard to understand why Miss Hannah had not been successful with her painting, for the dozen or so works Peggy showed me were exquisite – beautiful, detailed studies of birds, animals and flowers, executed in ink and watercolour. I remarked that I found them delightful and thought they could be valuable. I was about to suggest showing them to a dealer I knew when I was brought up short by the last painting, the only portrait. It was a sombre work compared with the nature studies, but had a compelling intensity. The grave, beautiful face that looked back at me belonged to Alice.

I asked Peggy whether she knew the identity of the sitter, but she replied that she had never taken much interest in the paintings and anyway liked flowers and animals better than people. Then I asked whether she had a photograph of Sybil Hannah, and she produced an old photo-album. 'No one else seemed to want it when she died, so I thought I'd take it rather than see it chucked out,' she explained. She turned the pages towards the end of the book and pointed out two ladies photographed in front of the carriage in the woods. 'I took that,' she said proudly. 'The older one's Sybil. The one with the cigarette is Cousin Phoebe. Neither of them got on ever so well with men.'

The last words were said meaningfully, and looking at the photograph I thought I caught the innuendo. Both ladies looked mannish and had their arms around each other's waists. Peggy went on:

'You can borrow the book if you want, and if it's of any interest you can still see old Phoebe. She lives in a bungalow out at Barrasford End.'

The album turned out to be a photographic chronicle of the Hannah family in its heyday. My heart leapt when I found, early on in the book, photographs of Alice and the young boy who had visited Santa with her. They were a year or so younger than when I had encountered them and in one picture they were accompanied by an older, rather plain, girl who looked sulky. Comparing this face with that of Sybil in later life I concluded that they belonged to the same person. From the captions I learnt that my Alice's real name was Emma and the small boy was called Stanley. However, Emma remained Alice to me.

The next day I paid a visit to Phoebe. I had telephoned her first to explain the purpose of my visit and she seemed in no way averse to meeting me. She was a brisk octogenarian who chain-smoked untipped cigarettes. The only damage this seemed to have caused her was a husky voice and occasional bouts of wheezy coughing. She was unembarrassed about her relationship with her cousin.

'Sybil was a very talented woman but very wary of other people. There had been a lot of tragedy in her life you know. Ken, her fiancé, was killed in the Great War, and later her father shot himself when the business crashed, but saddest of all she blamed herself for the deaths of her young brother and sister, and I think that her parents did as well, however much they tried to hide it.

'She only spoke of it once to me, and then only when she had put away the best part of a bottle of gin. Apparently what happened was that when she was about ten the family took themselves off on holiday. In those days the carriage you are interested in was used as a camping-coach. It stood in a lovely place by the sea on Anglesey, a siding off the main line just before Holyhead. She told me that one day the children sneaked out for an early-morning swim. It was barely light and the two youngest went running across the line and were hit by the Irish Mail. Poor Sybil, she couldn't really be blamed, but from then on everything went wrong for the Hannahs.'

I showed her the picture of the three children from the photo album. 'Is this them?' I asked.

The old lady's hand shook as she took the print.

'Yes, that's Sybil and her brother and sister all right. Sybil kept painting the girl, you know. She seemed almost to be haunted by the child.'

She looked at me directly as she said this, and I knew that she was expecting me to comment. I had to tell her of my own involvement in the saga. She did not seem surprised.

'Well, I never saw the pair myself but I know that Sybil often did. Those two were cruel to her when they were alive and were always getting her into trouble with her parents. Perhaps they were nasty enough to enjoy it, and even to carry on teasing her after death. But there is one other thing I ought to tell you now. The children got up early to escape the vigilance of their parents. They would dare each other to run across the line as near as they could to the trains. I think it's called "last across".'

'Is that why Sybil blamed herself?'

'Who can say all these years afterwards? She could have been so sick of their mischievousness that she wanted them to be hit by the train. But why should they appear to you? You've done them no wrong.'

I replied that I had thought a great deal on this subject. There was a theory, I explained, that ghosts emanated from the fabric of the place they haunted. Human emotions or suffering could be imprinted into the walls of a house (or in this case railway carriage) in much the same way as images on film or tape. An unknown kind of extra-sensory trigger could cause the appearance of a ghost. I said that all that remained to be done was to have the carriage exorcised.

The exorcism proved to be a simple, moving occasion

without any of the ballyhoo which is dreamed up by Hollywood. It was undertaken secretly – I did not want to tell my story to the committee! It will probably take many years before we can be certain that it has been successful, but I am encouraged that so far there have been no reports of anything untoward happening in the picnic-car; the jumble ladies are using it once more, and there does seem to be a warmer feeling to the coach, more in keeping with that of an old railway carriage now enjoying its well-earned retirement.

The Buckinghamshire Railway Centre is one of the largest railway preservation centres in the country. Steam trains operate on Sundays from Easter to October, and also on Wednesdays during the summer months. Coaches and coach-bodies (such as the saloon featured in 'Trouble with Alice') are on display, together with a very large collection of steam locomotives and other vintage railway equipment.

A derelict coach awaiting restoration

The Marmalade Tom

West Hoathly, even in its heyday, was never a busy station. It occupied an isolated position on the 'Bluebell and Primrose' line close to East Grinstead in Sussex. The nickname derived from the tradition that the trains went so slowly that passengers had time to pick bunches of wild flowers before running to board the train again. The station, with the famous Bluebell Inn which stood opposite, was some way to the north of the village, just beyond the portal of the tunnel which took the railway underneath its cottages. West Hoathly was always disliked by engine crews; going south they had to accelerate hard from a standstill up a 1 in 75 gradient to reach the tunnel, where the incline continued and adhesion was difficult on rails always wet and greasy.

In the early 1920s there was another reason to dislike West Hoathly – its stationmaster, John Murdoch.

Murdoch's face gave away much of his character. His features were dark and severe and his mouth had a bitter

The site of West Hoathly station showing the relaid track which is being steadily extended towards East Grinstead.

twist, as though he expected little from the world and received less. At one time he had been a pillar of the local Methodist church, but had left the small congregation after a row concerning the harvest festival, which he thought frivolous nonsense. Murdoch was a man of violent temper and abrasive tongue who ruled his family with a rod of iron. On first being appointed stationmaster he had attempted to impose the same form of harsh discipline on his subordinates. However, the isolation of the village (which meant that few railwaymen wished to move there) and the closeness of its people led to his being frustrated in this and then reprimanded by his superiors. After a week of the new regime, porters, clerks and signalmen had all made their minds known and put in for transfers. Since reports of his tyrannical behaviour were already circulating by way of visiting train crews, a quiet word was said and the onslaught against the staff (all of whom he regarded as lazy and slovenly) was ended.

There were still occasional outbursts of ungovernable rage against individuals, but on the whole he interfered little with the day-to-day running of the station, which virtually ran itself anyway, so light was its traffic.

Thus his temper and cruelty became focused on the family. Battered physically and verbally, his two sons escaped from home as soon as they could obtain jobs. His daughter, the only person for whom he seemed to hold any regard, fled at the age of fifteen, in the company of a young train guard. Then he was left alone in the station house with his wife, who was prematurely aged by her husband's behaviour. Her pale face and haunted, ever-restless eyes spoke of deep unhappiness, but although occasional sounds of violence reached beyond the walls of the house, the staff who heard them shrugged and went about their business.

One might think that it would have been easy for Mrs Murdoch to have fled as her children had done, but at that time women who left violent husbands were not treated with sympathy. In any case she had one consolation – her cats. None were allowed inside the house, but she fed all the strays of the district by the back door, ringing a little brass bell to tell them when it was feeding-time.

The cats – wily creatures – soon learned to avoid the lethal boots of the master of the house, although there were occasional casualties. Murdoch swore at the animals (good Methodist oaths!) but even his harshest efforts failed to stop his wife's caring for them.

Her particular favourite was a splendid marmalade tom she named Lucky. He was a faithful animal showing a real affection for her which was otherwise totally missing from her life. In the evenings she would sit on the platform seat furthest from the house, with the cat on her lap, until the last train came in at 9.15. Passengers getting off would nod and smile sympathetically at her, though she never acknowledged them.

Lucky was a cat of regular habits, and when he failed to turn up for his dinner at the usual time one sultry July evening Mrs Murdoch quickly became distracted. Taking the dish of cat-food she roamed about the station and its yard calling the cat's name and ringing the brass bell. She enquired after Lucky in the porters' room and the signalbox and walked the line a short way in each direction.

Dark storm-clouds brought dusk on quickly. John Murdoch appeared on the scene, enraged that his wife should be out seeking the cat rather than serving him with his supper. But she ran away from him towards the portal of the tunnel, ignoring his shouted threats and still calling 'Lucky! Lucky!' and ringing the bell.

Brighton Viaduct

LBSC station staff in the early years of the twentieth century

The stationmaster pursued her into the tunnel, only appearing to hesitate for a moment at its mouth. Then he vanished after her, swallowed up by the gloom.

Within a minute the signalman heard a long whistle-blast from the tunnel and a light engine, a small 0-6-0 tank, emerged from it and came to a standstill by his box. The engine-driver scrambled down from the cab and ran up the steps. 'I hit someone in the tunnel,' he said breathlessly, 'he was lying on the track.'

The signalman rang through on the telegraph to put a block on the line and sent the fireman to the station to organise a search party and lamps. When this was ready they walked back towards the tunnel, fearful of what they would find.

As they neared its mouth, the tinkling sound of a bell could be heard in the darkness and then a white shape appeared. Mrs Murdoch staggered out from the tunnel, still clutching the dish of cat-food. She looked at the men uncomprehendingly for a moment and then said, 'Are you looking for Lucky too?' Without waiting for an answer she walked back unsteadily towards the station and the dark clouds of the gathering storm.

They found Murdoch's body between the rails. The wheels of the loco had left it in a terrible state and it was clear that he had been killed instantly. But why had he been lying on the rails? This question later caused the coroner some concern before he came to the conclusion that Murdoch must have suffered a heart attack or died from a similar natural cause.

Mrs Murdoch was not at all affected by the death of her husband. She became calm on her return to the house, and carefully washed the kitchen knife that had been concealed in her apron pocket before returning it to its drawer. Lucky had been waiting for her at the kitchen door, and seemed to smile at her in a knowing way.

Lucky's mistress was given a pension which enabled her to rent a cottage perfect for her needs. She lived there, together with a host of cats, until the age of ninety, when she went to her grave a contented woman.

The entrance to the tunnel at West Hoathly

It was inevitable that West Hoathly should acquire a ghost after these events. Many spoke of the dark figure which would be seen roaming listlessly about the station, often standing by the northern portal of the tunnel. Permanent-way men disliked working inside, with the constant drip of water and the chance of glimpsing a terrible face, contorted by rage or fear. The other strange manifestation which has often been reported is the tinkle of a bell, often heard on evenings when there is thunder in the air.

When the Bluebell Railway opened for business in 1960 it was the first standard-gauge preserved railway in England. Of course at that time it was only natural that the trains should be steam-hauled, though the railway began with just two small locomotives and four-and-a-half miles of track between Sheffield Park and a point just short of Horsted Keynes.

The Bluebell now has more than thirty locos in its collection and a comprehensive array of rolling-stock. The line is being extended north towards Kingscote, on the outskirts of East Grinstead, a distance of more than eight miles from the southern terminus at Sheffield Park. The construction of the last two miles into East Grinstead will follow and bring about a connection with British Rail.

The Bluebell Railway was made a limited company in 1986 and, as befits its status as this country's senior preserved line, it runs a comprehensive service throughout the season and on Sundays in the winter. Special events include an autumn steam gala and children's fun weekend, while at the luxury end of the market the Golden Arrow Pullman offers the opportunity to wine and dine in the style of the 1920s.

Gwrach-y-rhibyn –
the Hag of the Night

The Royal Hotel was getting back to its pre-war standards, thought William Davidson as he climbed the stairs to his room. It had been an enjoyable evening at Llangollen where he had been playing host to the railway's important customers in the town – the woollen mill, seed company, coal merchants, and the farmers' cooperative. After the years of wartime austerity it was almost like old times to be served jugged hare (supplied by the stationmaster from an undisclosed source), and then go on to a fruit salad with real cream before finishing with excellent port and brandy from the GWR's directors' cellar, to which Davidson was privileged to have access.

With the end of the war in Europe it had been decided that the railway should make an effort to win back the goodwill of its pre-war customers, and this was the purpose of Davidson's visit to Llangollen. The spectre of competition from road transport had loomed over the company's freight operations in the years just before the outbreak of war; it was feared that this competition might grow now that hostilities had ended.

Davidson's stomach was still unused to such rich food, and when he reached his bedroom his first action was to rummage in his case for the blue bottle of Milk of Magnesia tablets that he kept for gastric emergencies. He soon found the bottle, but only one tablet was left inside and he knew he would inevitably spend a restless night. Angry with himself he walked to the window and looked down on the town. Thunder still rumbled around the hills and there were distant flashes of lightning. The rain poured down still, as it had done since early afternoon, and the Dee was in spate, the newly revived gas lights faintly illuminating its rushing waters.

Beyond the bridge he could see the station. As he watched, the duty-porter walked up the platform extinguishing the lamps, a cape thrown over his shoulders against the downpour. Davidson half-drew the curtains on the stormy night and undressed. Once in bed he soon fell into a sleep made uneasy both by his churning stomach and by the hot, thundery night.

Some time later he awoke, realising that a visit to the lavatory was becoming imperative. Still half-asleep he donned slippers and dressing-gown and walked unsteadily down the corridor to the bathroom. He returned shortly after, more comfortable but still half-asleep, and was about to get back into bed when he realised that he had forgotten to put his shoes outside the door for cleaning. As he retrieved them from the foot of the bed he heard a strange sound from just outside the window, a soft whoosh as though a large bird had passed close by at speed.

Davidson parted the curtains and looked out. Although thunder still rumbled it was more distant and the rain had stopped. The clouds parted for a moment and a full moon shone down on the scene. His attention was immediately drawn to a shadowy figure on the station platform. A strangely hunched shape looked a little like that of a bent-backed old woman. It was standing by the signal-box – but what could an old lady be doing on the station at such an hour? Davidson rubbed his eyes and when, a moment later, he looked again he saw that the creature had now stretched to its

A winter scene at Berwyn on the Llangollen Railway

full height and had unfolded an enormous pair of wings from its shoulders.

'This must be a dream,' he thought, shaking his head in an attempt to wake himself up. It made no difference, but in that moment the moon disappeared behind a cloud and the scene was dimmed. An instant later, moonlight bathed the landscape again: the station was empty but a weird shape glided above, silhouetted against the sky, its wings outstretched. Flapping them lazily, it flew off along the river, following it downstream towards the village of Trevor.

Davidson was now fully awake and pinched himself to make sure. Perhaps, he told himself, this was a waking dream where reality merges with the world of sleep. The moon had become screened by yet more storm-clouds, but a brilliant flash of lightning revealed that the station and the town now appeared empty of people or monsters. Davidson returned to his bed as loud thunder rolled over the vale. He slept, undisturbed by the continuing storm, until morning.

Davidson realised that something was amiss as soon as he drew the curtains. It was just before 7.30 and a train should have been standing at the station ready to leave for Wrexham with its usual clientèle of workpeople and schoolchildren. Plenty of people were thronging the station, but they appeared excited and confused, clustering round a porter at the entrance. Davidson shaved and dressed quickly and walked briskly over the bridge to the station. In the booking-hall he found the stationmaster, who broke away from a group of schoolchildren when he saw Davidson approaching.

'Goodness, Mr Davidson, sir,' he said, 'I'm afraid that in all the excitement I quite forgot you were here. There's bad news, the down Chester mail has been derailed at Sun Bank. The canal burst its bank and washed the line away.'

'Was anyone hurt?' asked Davidson.

'Just the driver, sir, and he's dead, or so I'm told. The train rolled down the embankment and it will take some days before the line's working again. Dreadful it is, sir, dreadful....'

Davidson often thought of his strange dream but never mentioned it until many years later, when his grandchildren began demanding creepy stories at bedtime. The tale of the 'flying grandma' became a great favourite, and one day his son-in-law, Gareth, who was Welsh, overheard him telling it. He interrupted:

'That's the Gwrach-y-rhibyn you're speaking of. She's a bit like a banshee who comes to warn when death's about, though it's more usual for her to visit the nobs who have lived in their stately homes or castles for generations. She beats her wings at the windows and you'll see her hideous face looking in. As you say, just like Grandma.'

This last remark earned him a wet dishcloth about the ears from his mother-in-law, but for all the outward frivolity the story remained in his mind because of more recent events which had unfolded at Llangollen.

Gareth had always been a railway enthusiast and he was a member of the Flint and Deeside Railway Preservation Society. In 1975 they had set about reinstating the track between Llangollen and Corwen, intending to run it as a steam line. He spent as much of his spare time as he could helping to get the railway running again. The team of workers came from all over England and Wales and were of widely different ages and backgrounds. None of the members was keener than Frank, an elderly former Great Western driver who also proved to have remarkable skill as a brickie.

Thus, soon after the society had taken over the lease on the trackbed, Frank and Gareth were in Berwyn tunnel replacing the brick facing of the western portal. It was a damp and gloomy job. Before they started Frank told Gareth the story of a policeman who once pursued a house-breaker into its smoky depths and was nearly mown down by a train. Presumably the robber escaped. He went on:

'It was a fearful place for engine crews too, specially in the old days when they had less protection in the cab and the locos were more likely to stall. It's a stiff climb up from Berwyn station on slippery rails. It was no joke for passengers either: if windows got left open the coaches would fill with smoke so you couldn't see across them, and the ladies would complain at their dresses being spoilt.

'What's more the tunnel is narrow, low and twisting, with bare rock only inches above the chimneys of big locos, so there was always the chance of a blow-back if you were rough on the regulator. We were careful to stand well back from the firebox door. Of course if you had an inspector or other unwelcome visitor on the footplate you could scare the hell out of him by leaving the door a little way open – he'd be hopping around like a madman by the time you reached daylight and there'd be cinder burns all over his trews!'

They worked together over several weekends replacing the rotting brickwork of the entrances, and when this was done they moved further inside the tunnel to repair the refuges where permanent-way men caught in the tunnel could shelter safely from passing trains.

Frank suddenly laid down his trowel and said that he was going out 'to get a spot of air'. Gareth thought little of this at the time though he was to reproach himself later.

He was working on alone when he suddenly felt a rush of chilly air on his face. For a terrible moment he imagined a train was rushing towards him, but what brushed past him was hardly less horrible. An unearthly creature flapped its way down the tunnel leaving a putrid smell in its wake ('like rugger-socks at full time' was how Gareth later described it). Its silhouette framed by the end of the tunnel was like that of a huge, ungainly, slow-moving bat.

Gareth ran out of the tunnel, stumbling on the rough trackbed. He found Frank lying huddled up just beyond the portal and felt for a pulse, even though he knew it would be in vain – the Gwrach-y-rhibyn never made a mistake....

They held a wake for Frank, members of the society thinking that their old colleague would have appreciated the gesture. About a dozen members were still present at closing-time at the Jenny Jones. By that time Gareth had put down several pints and he saw no point in holding back the story of the apparition he had seen in the tunnel. For good measure he told of his father-in-law's dream as well, endowing it with all of his Celtic sense of the dramatic. No one spoke when he finished, but after a moment someone broke the spell with a facetious comment: 'We could make it a selling-point. The only preserved line with a ghost – or is it a vampire! The Hag of the Tunnel – I see it now in the *Sun*. Allan here would make a good hag, wouldn't you, son, dressed up in your biker's gear and wings!'

A 'Thomas the Tank Engine' Special pulls away from Berwyn on the Llangollen Railway

He threw an arm about the largest member in the group, who grinned back sheepishly, conscious of being overweight by a stone or three. Gareth said, his words now slurred, 'It's not wise to mock, you know. It might bring her back.'

Work continued on the restoration of the railway, and 1981 saw the running of the first steam train along a short stretch of track. Later the railway was extended to Berwyn and then to Deeside Junction. In 1992 the track was restored as far as Glyndyfrdwy, nearly six miles from Llangollen. Corwen seemed within easy reach to the band of cheerful and enthusiastic volunteers. The Hag of the Tunnel had passed into the folklore of the society, the story by now embellished with so much extra detail that it sounded more like a fairytale.

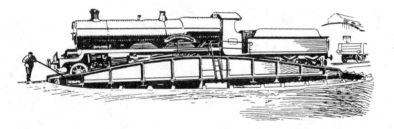

Gareth himself was now in late middle age and with his children grown up was able to spend even more time at Llangollen. He was on the main committee, had a major shareholding in one of the locos and often did firing turns.

It was after one of these that disaster struck. The loco had been used for a Thomas the Tank Engine event and he was preparing to drop the fire. He had moved the engine over the ash pit and was beneath it with a long fire-iron raking the ash and clinker out from its grate. He never heard the shout of warning as wagons loaded with granite chippings escaped from the maintenance train and began to roll down the slight gradient towards him. His attention had already been taken by a sound he had heard many years earlier, the lazy flap of leathern wings.

The impact of the wagons with the loco threw the engine back. The fire-iron was driven deep into Gareth's chest and he was pinned by it in the slurry of ash and clinker at the bottom of the pit. He was quickly senseless and didn't see or hear the departure of the Gwrach-y-rhibyn as she flew into the deepening gloom over the Llangollen rooftops.

The revival of the railway between Llangollen and Corwen began in 1972, four years after British Railways abandoned the line. Initially Llangollen station and about three miles of track westwards were leased from the council and work began on refurbishing the station.

In 1975 Llangollen station was opened to the public, though it was not until 1981 that the first passenger train ran from its platform. Also in 1981, the society obtained a lease on the ten miles of trackbed to Corwen.

At first trains only ran a very short distance, but gradually the route has been extended, most significantly to Glyndyfrdwy in 1992. It is hoped that a service to Corwen will be running by 1995.

An excellent array of locos can be seen working at Llangollen, headed by Great Western 7822, Foxcote Manor. Engines are often brought from other societies to augment those based at Llangollen, so that there is always something new and interesting to see.

Few preserved railways run through more glorious scenery, and the gradients of the route provide a stiff challenge for both the locos and their crews. Trains run at weekends from early spring to mid-May, when a daily service begins. This lasts throughout the summer until late September. There are also special events such as Thomas the Tank Engine weekends and the usual Santa Specials before Christmas.

The Black Crow

It was natural for Tom Applegarth to be at the shed early as the next day would be an important one for him. He was booked for his first main-line firing duty. Through the gloom he could dimly see an array of imposing engines grouped around the turntable. Highly polished brass caught the gleam of the flickering gaslights and there was just a hint of rich maroon paintwork. Somewhere inside there was a sudden loud clang as though a spanner or fire-iron had been dropped, but Tom knew that the noise was more likely to have been caused by the contraction of some part of a loco's mechanism as it cooled. Or, of course, it might be 'Weary Willie', the slow-moving hunched figure who was supposed to haunt the Hellifield shed.

The engine Tom was seeking was unlikely to be inside the shed, however. A few weeks previously it had been his task as cleaner to prepare locos for their day's work: now that hard and often unpleasant job was done by someone else and he was entitled to moan to the foreman if things were not as they should be when he reached the footplate.

He left the shed and walked out into the driving rain towards the coaling-stage where he expected to find his loco – No. 1010, a 3-cylinder Johnson Compound, practically brand-new from the Midland Railway's Derby works. Although he knew that its duties would be humble on this trip (piloting an express goods northwards from Hellifield to the summit of the Settle and Carlisle line at Ais Gill) he had never fired so celebrated a machine before. The Settle and Carlisle was regarded with awe by firemen from other companies, for 'The Long Drag' was a fireman's Matterhorn, a test of skill and stamina. Many newly passed stokers had suffered the indignity of having their shovels snatched away from them at crucial moments by the driver as strength flagged and the needle dropped in the pressure gauge.

Tom had been rostered to this duty early in his career for two reasons. The driver's regular mate, 'Irish' Cunningham, a usually good-natured giant of a man, had taken himself back to his homeland after a fight with his wife and an epic three-day drinking-bout (not necessarily in that order). Furthermore it was Christmas time (the greater part of this shift would fall on Christmas Eve), when sudden indisposition often mysteriously afflicted the workforce.

He pulled himself up onto the footplate. The cab provided welcome shelter from the downpour, though the gale blasted across the open space between tender and cab. Tom looked at the gauges – the pressure was well up and the glass showed plenty of water in the boiler. Opening the firebox door he saw a good even fire blazing inside. The cleaner had done his job well. The burnished brass of the controls shone brightly in the firelight and he was well satisfied. He checked to make sure that all the fire-irons were safely stacked on the tender, then filled his shovel from the bunker; the coal looked good too. Tom threw the shovelful to the back of the firebox and then, a glance at his watch having confirmed that it was now twenty minutes past midnight on Christmas Eve, he peered out into the darkness looking for his driver, Clarence Enwright.

'Little Salkeld' – one of the stations on the Settle and Carlisle line near Penrith. A southbound overnight express begins its climb to Ais Gill.

In the distance, coat pulled tightly at the collar against the rain which was being driven horizontally by the gale, a figure could be seen struggling towards the engine. Tom felt a slight tingle of apprehension – Clarence was a driver of the old school who had the reputation of dealing shortly with young firemen. He grunted a greeting to Tom as he heaved himself aboard the loco, and then spat a juicy mouthful of well-chewed tobacco out of the cab.

'Look, son, I could have done without you. You keep out of my hair and I'll not trouble you as long as you keep the steam up. You'll have no breath to talk with once we're on the road, but if you do want an answer you'll call me "sir". Right?'

Tom nodded diffidently in reply and Clarence moved the engine forward to take on water, the young fireman having to climb onto the tender in order to put the heavy leather bag of the water-column into the tank. He came back to the cab soaked and frozen, rubbing his hands.

Clarence spat again into the darkness as he moved the loco forward to the signal which protected the main line. Tom was busy building his fire and the gauge was showing a healthy pressure, the safety valve just beginning to lift.

'Open the injectors and keep that bloody noise down', shouted Clarence, 'or it'll be waking my missus.' Close by were rows of Midland Railway cottages. Tom glanced at the driver's face, thinking he had caught a hint of humour in his tone, but Clarence's features held their usual scowl.

1010 was signalled into a siding on the up line to await the arrival of the goods train which they would help to haul over the steep section of the line to Ais Gill. After about forty minutes a whistle hooted and the lights of a loco could be seen approaching slowly. The signal at the siding came off, and Clarence slowly eased the Compound onto the main line and then backed down to the waiting train. Tom jumped from the cab and coupled 1010 to the train engine, which proved to be another Compound. 'How many wagons?' he shouted to its driver.

He just managed to hear the reply – fifty-eight closed wagons, all laden. A tidy size, but there should be no problems with the load even in these conditions. By the time he reached the cab the starter signal had dropped, and when the train

A Compound waits for its next duty at Ais Gill

engine whistled Clarence pulled on his whistle-chain and opened the regulator. The engine surged forward momentarily before being checked by the weight of the load behind. The driver applied the sander as wheels slipped on the wet rails – the battle against the gradient had been joined. Tom would be shifting at least half a ton of coal from tender to firebox over the next twenty miles. His shirt was already soaked with sweat.

Possibly 1010 had shown signs of the 'black crow' which sat upon its dome before this (a black crow is a jinx in railwaymen's parlance), but it was this occasion which laid the foundation of the legend. At Horton-in-Ribblesdale they were set back into the siding to await the passing of the up Scottish express. The double-headed express thundered through after about ten minutes, and almost immediately the light changed as they were signalled back onto the main line.

Again Clarence tugged at the whistle-chain to announce to the train-crew that they were about to start their journey again. But this time there was not just the usual deep 'toot':

when he let go of the chain the whistle continued to blow – its valve had jammed and the steam sent out an endless note into the stormy night. Clarence stood nonplussed for a moment but then shouted to Tom: 'Turn that valve,' pointing to a cock high up on the fireman's side of the bulkhead.

Obediently Tom moved towards it and tried to move the tap clockwise. He put all his strength into it, double-handed, but still could not budge it, and the steam went on through the whistle to make an ever more deafening din.

There was a sudden jolt as the engine behind attempted to start the train on its own – to no avail since Clarence had not released the brakes.

'Get out of the way and let me have a go,' he shouted, and pushed Tom back to wrestle with the obdurate valve himself. After a moment he swore an obscene oath and picked up the coal hammer. Even a series of hefty clouts with this brought no success.

'You'd better go back and tell the sods behind what's happened,' he yelled at Tom. 'We'll try to get up to Hawes and then fix it when we drop off this train. You'd best tell the guard and the bobby too.'

The young fireman could only do what he was told, hoping that Clarence would have the decency to keep a good fire on the engine. Having told the other driver of their predicament he stumbled back along the length of the train to inform the guard, and borrowed a lantern from him to light his way to the signal-cabin, whose glow he could just make out from the end of the train. Here the shrieking of the wind over the desolate moors completely drowned the sound of the whistle.

'I was wondering what you were up to,' said the signalman. 'You'll be lucky to make Blea Moor, though, if you're losing steam like that. I'll telegraph ahead and let them know what to expect. I can give you a clear road anyway.'

Tom thanked him and made his way back to the pilot engine as quickly as he could. He was pleased to find that Clarence had kept the pressure up with a hot fire, although the whistle was still blowing. Tom waved his lantern from the cab and the two engines synchronised their start, getting the heavy train out onto the main line without difficulty.

The pressure which had registered on the gauge at the start

soon began to fall back alarmingly as they continued their climb. Tom fired like a maniac, but the pace of the train faltered and was soon down to below twenty miles an hour, and still the pressure dropped. The loss of steam through the jammed whistle was just enough to tilt the battle against the gradient in the latter's favour. However, deliverance was at hand – at Dent they were stopped by the signal. The bobby emerged from his signal-box and ran towards them.

'You'll have to get out of the road,' he shouted, 'the Scottish express has ploughed into a pair of light engines by Moorcock Tunnel and the whole wreck's ablaze. There's a special on its way up from Settle now.' He added as an afterthought: 'And can't you stop that bloody noise – we've got enough trouble as it is.'

In truth the whistle was quieter now than it had been before, when it had more steam behind it. Nevertheless it took Clarence, helped by the driver from the other train and a crowbar, another ten minutes before the valve turned and it was finally silenced. Soon afterwards a short train carrying doctors and policemen went by. Clarence scowled at Tom, spat another stream of tobacco juice, and said, 'I don't know whether it's you or this bloody loco that's the Jonah, but one is, that's for sure. I'm not going to have anything else to do with either of you if I can help it.'

Soon after this Tom was transferred to another shed, but he still kept an ear open for gossip about 1010 in canteens and clubs. Her career continued to consist of a series of break-downs and misadventures. When, just three years later, he heard that there had been another accident at Ais Gill he fully expected 1010 to have been involved. At first sight, however, it seemed that she had managed to avoid playing a part in the tragedy; later he found that she had, indirectly, done so.

It was probably sheer coincidence that 1010 was at Carlisle shed on that fateful September night in 1913. She was standing waiting for her driver, looking immaculate in her smart Midland livery. Sam Caudle had an affection for the engine and relished her bad reputation. He preferred driving her to any other loco on the shed, and because of his seniority (plus the fact that no one else wanted to risk his reputation with such a beast of ill omen) he was usually on her footplate.

Who knows what his fate would have been had he been able to take her out as planned, but as he approached the engine, Follows, the young fireman who had been booked with him for this shift, hurried towards him with a worried expression.

'Mr Caudle, the footplate's missing on the engine.'

The driver was at first inclined to pour scorn on this statement, but when he climbed the steps he found the complaint was justified. The wooden boards which usually covered the gap between bunker and cab had been burnt away. Whether this had occurred during the previous working or had happened subsequently in the shed was immaterial. Obviously there was urgent need for a relief engine, as they were booked for an important duty – the overnight express from Edinburgh, due to depart from Carlisle at 1.49 that morning. Caudle made for the superintendent's office.

He found another agitated crew already there claiming the relief engine as a pilot. 'Nick' Nicholson, though lacking Caudle's seniority, was a respected driver at Carlisle and was putting his point forcibly. He too was down to drive a night express, in this case the Stranraer boat-train which would be joined with carriages from Glasgow at Carlisle. He had discovered that the combined train would weigh thirteen tons over the limit set for his loco. Furthermore his tender had been loaded with very poor coal, from a new supply which was full of slack and clinkered easily. He very much doubted whether his engine, a Class 4 4-4-0, would make it over the Ais Gill summit without assistance.

Caudle looked at him scornfully, envious of the younger man's reputation as an up-and-coming 'link' driver.

'Of course you'll make it if you're any good. I've taken trains over there that have been fifty tons over the limit. Any road, you'll have to tonight, because we have to take the relief. There's nothing else here that can haul the Edinburgh.'

The superintendent had to agree with this, and both crews trudged back to their locos. It was a windy night, but a dry one, so at least there would be no wet rails to trouble them.

Follows found that the same poor coal was loaded on their tender. 'Yes,' said Caudle, 'it's rubbish all right just as Nick said. We'll just have to make do though, like we will with this Class 2. All you have to do is to keep a clean fire. I reckon you'll have a grate full of clinker when we reach Leeds.'

He was dismayed to learn from Follows that this was the first time the young fireman had worked on a Class 2, but hoped that his own years of experience would help them over any difficulties.

Driver Nicholson was not so confident of his chances of reaching the Ais Gill summit. There had been a reasonable fire in the box at the shed, but even as he backed the engine onto its train at Citadel Station it was looking dull at the bottom.

'Keep stirring it up,' he said to his fireman as he switched on

An express diverted from the West Coast main line approaches the Ais Gill summit

the blower. But he knew that the latter could hardly rake and shovel at the same time, and feared the start of the 1 in 100 gradient after Ormside.

Sure enough, speed was lost quickly on the long ascent, and although the driver took a turn with the shovel himself they came to an enforced halt about half a mile from the summit, when the steam pressure became insufficient to hold the vacuum brake off.

When the front train-guard came to ask how long they were likely to be delayed Nicholson shouted into the wind: 'We'll be a few minutes.' This was relayed to the rear guard as 'only a minute', and so, fatally, the latter did not consider it worth while to walk back and put down warning detonators.

Caudle and Follows had left Carlisle with the Edinburgh express fifteen minutes after Nicholson. They too had trouble in raising steam and when, approaching Birkall Tunnel, Caudle left the cab with his oil can to top up the axle-boxes, they were losing speed. Because of the gusting wind he was longer topping up than usual, and by the time he returned to the cab they were past the Mallerstang distant. This signal stood at danger, and the inexperienced fireman failed to see it: he was having trouble with the injector. Caudle moved across the footplate to help him because the situation was rapidly becoming critical, with water only just showing in the bottom of the glass.

Approaching Mallerstang signal-box the train was travelling slowly and the signalman thought its driver must be taking heed of the distant and was prepared to stop at the next signal. Thus he lowered his home signal but kept the starter at danger. As the express came closer he was dismayed to see that it was now picking up speed and was about to ignore the danger signal. Frantically he waved a lamp from the balcony but the driver and fireman were still preoccupied with the injector and failed to see either him or the signal. Moments later Follows, glancing ahead through the window, shouted: 'Look out, Sam, there's a red light ahead!'

At first the driver thought that this was the Ais Gill distant and gave a whistle-blast, hoping it would be lowered. In fact the red light was the tail-lamp of the stalled express from Glasgow, and Caudle was only about 200 yards away from it when he realised his error. There was barely time to shut off steam.

Driver Nicholson watched the nightmare unfold. The glowing firebox of the other train was the first intimation of disaster. Despairingly he tugged at the whistle-chain and opened the regulator, but there still wasn't sufficient pressure to release the brakes. The impact of the Edinburgh express with the rear of the Glasgow train was devastating. The last two coaches were smashed to pieces, the roof of one landing on the leading Edinburgh coach and tearing it open. Caudle's engine was completely buried in the wreckage, which quickly began to smoulder and then burst into flames.

Remarkably both Caudle and Follows survived the accident, in which sixteen passengers died. The inquest held that four people were to blame for the accident – Caudle, his fireman, the rear guard, and the loco superintendent at Carlisle (for not supplying Nicholson with a pilot). Caudle was subsequently tried for manslaughter and found guilty, but the Midland Railway were more merciful: they paid his wages for the brief time of his captivity and gave him his job back afterwards.

Although the role of 1010 had been a passive one in this accident, there is no doubt that her incapacity triggered the subsequent events. Tom Applegarth maintained an interest in her career through the years. He heard of another instance of her whistle jamming. She was brought to a stop by an over-keen signalman who knew his working practices (a continuous note on the whistle is an alarm call in railway operations, and in these circumstances a signalman working to the rule book should stop and inspect the train).

Unfortunately a Midland Railway director was on the train at the time, and his anger at the delay, which caused him the humiliation of arriving late at an inter-railway meeting, cost the loco, its crew and the signalman dear. The careers of the railwaymen concerned withered from this time, which also marked the end of 1010 working express traffic (a punishment which could have come from the pages of Rev Awdry).

Other minor incidents continued to plague it up to, and even after, nationalisation. It once overran signals to hit the rear of a standing train of furniture containers. Although little damage was done to the engine or even to other rolling-stock, the valuable furniture suffered badly and the accident led to an enormous insurance claim. During the war it ran over a land mine dropped near Coventry and miraculously remained on the tracks after the explosion, though both men on the footplate were killed. Not surprisingly, when it was at last towed off for scrap no preservation society showed interest in saving it from the cutter's torch.

The Settle and Carlisle line has long been a mecca for steam enthusiasts. Steam trains may still be seen thundering up to Ais Gill summit, though each now has two firemen – a practice which must amuse veteran stokers. The old Ais Gill signal-box, which must hold psychic echoes of the terrible happenings there in 1913, may be seen at Butterley, where the Midland Railway Centre has rolling-stock and artefacts which bring to life the working of the Midland in its heyday. The only Midland Compound to be preserved (No. 1000) is at the National Railway Museum at York.

The Settle and Carlisle line is not preserved except in the sense that, had it not been for the pressure generated by railway-lovers, British Rail would have closed it some years ago. On weekends when there are steam workings, enthusiasts jostle for trackside viewpoints: the sight and sound of an A4 or similar express engine cresting the Ais Gill summit provide an incomparable experience. Let's hope that it continues for as long as main-line trains run in Britain.

The Red Dawn

Field Marshal Horatio Herbert Kitchener, 1st Earl of Khartoum and of Broome, Secretary of State for War and probably the most famous and popular man in Britain after the monarch, marched purposefully down the platform at King's Cross. A handful of soldiers and sailors on the train noticed his unmistakable face and raised a cheer. No flicker of acknowledgement crossed his face as he strode on, the station-master in frock-coat and top-hat vainly attempting to retain his dignity as his short legs tried to keep up with Kitchener's brisk strides. In front of the special coach attached to the afternoon Edinburgh express an agitated figure awaited their arrival.

'Mr O'Beirne, what ails you?' the Field Marshal enquired of the pale, worried-looking man.

'My lord, it's Matthews, my clerk. It appears that he has not yet arrived, and he has the ciphers with him. I have tele-phoned my office and it seems he may have gone to London Bridge by mistake.'

'Well, we cannot hold the train longer. Stationmaster, will you please arrange to have a special train and a clear line ready for Mr O'Beirne and his clerk, when he arrives. It must make all speed to catch us at York.' Kitchener turned to say farewell to those of his staff who had come to King's Cross to see him off. 'Look after things while I am away,' he said as they slammed the door.

It was an inauspicious start to the mission, reflected Detective Inspector Graham, Kitchener's regular bodyguard, who was assigned to the party whilst it was still on the main-land. By nature suspicious, he wondered how anyone could be so ignorant as to go to London Bridge to take a train to the north.

Ten minutes after their arrival in York the 'special' arrived with O'Beirne and his clerk. Graham noticed with satisfaction that their complexions wore a distinctly greenish hue. Their headlong journey was to become a legend on the east-coast main line, the driver of the Atlantic engine involved – the

An atmospheric study of a Highland Railway express hauled by loco No. 144, Blair Castle

King's Cross pilot – subsequently becoming known as Dick Turpin.

As the whistle blew for their departure from York, Graham pulled the window up and began his patrol of the length of the train, carefully locking the connecting door of the special coach behind him. How typical of the man, he thought, to use a scheduled service instead of a requisitioned 'special'. Kitchener was always worrying about the nation's resources and was also famous for his meanness. So, instead of a comfortable eleven-hour doze from London to Edinburgh, Graham was on his feet for almost all of the time. Whenever the locomotive stopped he had to be on his guard, and in between times he patrolled up and down to make sure there was no renegade passenger aboard who might have assassination in mind.

Graham was one of the very few people who shared any sort of intimacy with Kitchener. The latter seemed aloof, even arrogant, to many who served him and never suffered fools gladly. Early on the Field Marshal had discovered that Graham had served under him with the Highland Brigade in South Africa, and on the rare occasions when they had to spend time alone together Kitchener seemed to enjoy reminiscing. Graham looked forward to these times and hoped that his long journey might provide such an opportunity.

After leaving Newcastle Kitchener and his staff took a late dinner in the dining-car. The handful of other diners looked in awe at the great man, who seemed absorbed in his own thoughts and spoke little at table. They arrived at Edinburgh's Waverley Station in the small hours. Their special train, which included a sleeping-coach, was standing at an adjacent platform. Within minutes baggage was exchanged between the two trains and the journey resumed.

Lord Kitchener's trip to Russia was meant to be a top-secret mission but it is likely that, so leaky was the security in Russia, the Germans knew about it even before his train left King's Cross. The Russians needed reassurance that supplies would reach them so that the fight in the east might go on. Kitchener, Britain's war-lord, was the man to take encouragement to the Tsar. It would be fatal for the Allies if Russia crumbled, and the morale of her troops was already being undermined by the revolutionary efforts of the Bolsheviks. It was planned that the *Hampshire*, a cruiser freshly returned to Scapa Flow from the indecisive Battle of Jutland, should carry Kitchener and his party to Archangel. The train would take them to Thurso and then they would embark at nearby Scrabster for the short voyage to the Orkneys. They would set sail from Scapa Flow in the *Hampshire* in the afternoon, about fifteen hours after leaving Edinburgh.

With the rest of the party retired to their sleeping-berths, Kitchener sat alone in the saloon as the train rattled northwards, the timbre from the rails changing as it crossed the Forth Bridge. He was thinking of the keenness shown by Asquith and the other politicians that he should make the trip, and knew that it arose as much from their eagerness to undermine his position during his absence as from a desire for the mission to be successful. He knew that he had enemies within the government who were jealous of his friendship with the King and his popularity with the British people. It would be convenient for them if an accident happened – a train crash perhaps, or a torpedo sinking his ship in the Arctic Ocean.

He dozed fitfully, images from the past flickering through the margins of consciousness. Scenes from boyhood in Ireland,

where his tyrannical father was hated by his tenants and
neighbours; later years struggling with academic subjects at a
Swiss boarding school, and then as a cadet at Woolwich. There
was his carpeting by the Duke of Cambridge, when he was
severely reprimanded for having briefly joined with the
French army in 1871 to fight against the Prussians. After this,
success began to come his way in the army, and the memories
were thus now more congenial ones; among them were
episodes from the campaigns in Egypt and South Africa.
Suddenly, however, began the dream that he always feared.
He was struggling in water and it was about to close over his
head....

'Are you all right, my lord? I heard you cry out just now.'

Inspector Graham was regarding him with an anxious expression.

'Yes, of course. I was dreaming, that's all.' Kitchener looked round for the tunic which he had apparently stripped off during the course of his nightmare.

'Sorry if I disturbed you, my lord, I'm just on my rounds,' Graham said as he made to leave.

'How far have we got, Graham? I see that the sky is lightening.'

'We'll be stopping at Pitlochry in a moment for water, sir,' the policeman answered, his words being confirmed a moment later when the brakes were applied.

'I think I'll take a breath of fresh air here – will you join me?' said Kitchener as they drew up to the water column at the end of the platform.

The engine-crew glanced at the two men curiously as they stepped onto the platform, but quickly resumed their task when they saw that they were being watched. The air was cold and the reddish glow in the east heralded the June dawn.

'You're a Scotsman are you not, Graham? Do you come from these parts?'

'Aye, sir,' Graham replied, putting on a heavy accent. 'Our clan once found fame in this glen.'

'You'd best tell me about it then – it will pass a few miles,' Kitchener said as they boarded the carriage again and took their seats.

'Well, I can't lay claim to being of the nobility,' continued Graham, 'but it was my namesake John Graham of Claverhouse, Viscount Dundee, who led the Scots against the English at Killiecrankie and overran them. William's army was sent packing by the Highlanders – a rare enough occurrence. We'll be coming up to Killiecrankie Pass in a minute, sir, where the burn is supposed to have run red with the blood of the English dead, cut down as they fled.' Graham ended his story with some relish.

Both men looked out of the window. The light was strengthening but had a strange, unworldly quality about it. The gorge and its surroundings were suffused in a crimson glow, almost as though blood had been spilled over the carriage windows. Graham gave a shudder.

'It must have been like this on the day of the battle,' he said, almost to himself.

Kitchener looked at him directly with piercing blue eyes. 'Go on then, man, tell the whole story.'

'There's strange tales told about the battle, sir. How there was a strange red sky like this on the day it took place. Bonnie Dundee, that's Graham of Claverhouse, had been troubled by a dream the night before. A phantom had come to his tent as he slept, a man whose head was spouting blood from a terrible wound. He led Dundee out of his tent and pointed down to Killiecrankie where the two armies would meet. This happened three times and Dundee took it to be an omen of disaster. He told his closest lieutenant of the incident and made him swear to keep it a secret should the battle be lost. But the bold Highlanders won, and Dundee was rejoicing in their pursuit of the English when he was struck by a stray shot and fell, mortally wounded. There's all sorts of stories too about how you can see the battle sometimes, and even hear the shouts and screams of the soldiers as well as the musket volleys. I've met a shepherd who swears he's seen and heard the battle here.'

Both men continued to stare through the window at the scene where the massacre had occurred two centuries ago. The Field Marshal spoke without taking his eyes from the landscape: 'I find that a peculiarly disturbing story, Inspector Graham. I would hate to think of the suffering endured in battle being repeated.'

The train was moving slowly now as it swung round a sharp curve high above the river. Kitchener turned away from the window to look directly at his bodyguard.

'I take it that there are instances of similar phenomena elsewhere? Do we not pass by Culloden Moor on this route? Does such an event take place there?' Although Kitchener's face, half hidden by the immense moustache, maintained its habitual stern impassiveness, Graham thought he detected the slightest hint of a tremor in the voice.

'There is indeed, sir, supposed to be a haunting at Culloden, but it is hardly surprising for that too is an eerie and desolate spot where a terrible massacre took place. The lifeblood of the nation was drained there....'

He stopped, fearing that his sympathy for the Jacobite cause would not have gone down well with Kitchener. But the great man seemed distracted by thoughts of his own.

'I find it interesting that a place can hold captive the ghastly spectre of war, though I have heard that something similar has recently been reported from France. To control the destiny of thousands of men is a momentous responsibility: I fear that it is a burden which is beginning to haunt *me*. Mr Graham, I do not wish to pass by the battlefield of Culloden.'

Kitchener's decision not to proceed on the direct line to Inverness was received with consternation by the Highland Railway officials when it was relayed from Dalwhinnie. Both the direct line and the alternative via Forres were heavily loaded with traffic from the north, and a road for the special train had been carefully arranged to avoid hold-ups at passing loops. The reason for the heavy traffic was the number of ambulance trains proceeding southwards, bearing casualties from the ships hit or sunk during the Battle of Jutland. It was planned that the distinguished travellers on the special train should breakfast at Aviemore, where the engine would be changed and the journey resumed after twenty minutes or so. The change of route which Kitchener had demanded meant that one of the two ambulance trains on the Forres line would have to be brought forward to Aviemore, where it would cross with Kitchener's train while he was breakfasting. The ambulance train was not meant to stop there, but pass through onto the main line to take on water at Kingussie, the next station to the south. Its driver was proud of his loco, No. 224, which belonged to the North British and was famous for having been salvaged from the bed of the Tay in 1879, after the bridge collapsed with No. 224 and its train almost in the middle. For this the loco was nicknamed 'The Diver'. It now stopped at the water column, its carriages directly opposite the tearoom where Kitchener's party were at breakfast.

A fine spread had been laid out for breakfast and an appetising aroma drifted over the station. Two waiters from Inverness had been brought to Aviemore to serve the meal. Kippers, haddock and trout were decoratively presented on one salver. Another held scrambled eggs and kedgeree while a third displayed kidneys, bacon and black pudding. Porridge

A heavy Highland Railway train photographed at Dingwall – the name of the leading engine is Ben Armin

steamed gently in a tureen, a large jug of cream standing close by. Looking through the window of his carriage Stoker Davies, late of HMS *Lion*, saw this repast and then the group of nobs walking towards it. He didn't recognise any of the party at

first, as the stationmaster and his staff were doing their best to hide the ambulance train from view. However, at the last moment, just as he was about to enter the refreshment room, Kitchener looked to his right and glimpsed the train. His gaze met the stare of Stoker Davies's remaining eye, which instantly recognised the face behind the pointing finger on posters which had jolted the consciences of two-and-a-half million men and helped in drawing them to the recruiting centres.

'Bastard,' he said under his breath, and then, more loudly, 'murdering bastard!' as he lowered himself from his bunk and, grabbing his crutches, made for the door of the carriage, which had been left open.

His arrival in the refreshment room was dramatic. A swaying, half-naked figure swathed in bandages, he paused at the entrance for a moment as his eye searched for the man he felt to be responsible for the calamities that had befallen him. It is human nature to seek a scapegoat, and Kitchener served his purpose perfectly.

'Bastard!' He shouted the word this time as he spotted the Field Marshal seated at a table. 'This is what you've done to me!' Regardless of the pain he tore the bandages away from his face, revealing the marbled mess of torn flesh which had replaced his features. 'You and your bloody war!'

With this cry he lurched towards Kitchener, one crutch upraised. It was at that moment that Graham shot him. As he went down his scarred hands grabbed at the tablecloth, pulling dishes and cutlery to the floor. He held Kitchener's eye with his own for a long moment before it became unfocused and sightless and his head dropped.

The sailor's attack on Kitchener and his consequent death were one of the better-kept secrets of the war. Badly shaken, the mission continued its progress to Caithness. A storm was brewing when they embarked in the fleet drifter which took them out to the *Hampshire*. The storm had grown in strength by the time the cruiser sailed at 4.45 pm, and soon afterwards the easterly gale backed, so that the *Hampshire* and her escorts were offered no protection from the shore of the Orkney mainland. The destroyer escorts were forced to turn back leaving the *Hampshire*, steaming at eighteen knots, to make her way round the steepling cliffs of Marwick Head alone.

It was at 7.30 pm that she struck the mine which had been laid by a German submarine two weeks previously. There was little chance of survival for any crew or passengers. One or two life-rafts with sailors clinging to them managed to reach tiny, safe inlets beneath the great cliffs, but most of the ship's complement went down with her. Kitchener was one of them, last seen standing unperturbed on the bridge next to the captain. His death stunned the nation, and the mysteries surrounding it have occupied the writers of succeeding generations. Although Kitchener's spirit seems to have been content with his watery grave, at Aviemore another ghost continues to haunt the windswept platforms on stormy nights. It is the apparition of a faceless man, wrapped in bandages, who is heard to mutter 'Bastard, you murdering bastard!' as he lurches along on his crutches.

The Strathspey Railway was formed in 1971 to reopen five miles of former Highland Railway main line between Aviemore and Boat of Garten.

The line was first opened in 1863, and closed in 1968. Restoration consumed a great deal of time and money but in 1978 steam trains once again made the journey between Boat of Garten and Aviemore. 1992 will see the first real signs of the reconstruction of the line between Boat of Garten and Grantown-on-Spey, when the road bridge at Boat of Garten is replaced.

The steam railway operates a train service between Easter and the end of October. During the main summer months a daily service is operated; intending passengers should obtain a timetable from the railway.

Included in the fleet of locomotives are 5025, an LMS 'Black Five' of 1934 which once worked over the Highland main line, and 828, an ex-Caledonian Railway locomotive built at St Rollox, Glasgow, in 1899. There is also an ex-British Railways 2-6-0 of 1952, several 'Austerity' tanks, and a number of industrial locomotives from Andrew Barclay of Kilmarnock. Normally the railway operates one locomotive from the three or four in working order.

Arley Castle

My paper round brought me in enough money for my Runabout Ticket. It amazes me now when I think of the freedom enjoyed by a thirteen-year-old back in 1954. The Runabout took me all on my own to far-distant extremities of the former GWR and LMS at an incredibly cheap rate. It covered all the railways of a large area, though you had to avoid the main lines at peak times. Usually I journeyed alone, but occasionally with like-minded friends, our haversacks filled with sandwiches and bottles of Corona, pockets bulging with Ian Allan reference books, timetables and notebooks. If more than one of our group bought a Runabout ticket we might have a competition to see who could cover the greatest distance in the five days – once I managed just over 2,000 miles, most of it on branch-lines. Wherever I went I carried my father's battered pre-war Rolleiflex and a tripod – I wanted to be a photographer when I grew up and felt very honoured to be trusted with the lovely old camera.

We lived at Edgbaston in Birmingham so I could hardly have been in a better position to explore railways. My favourite direction, though, was westwards towards the quiet countryside that lies along the border with Wales. There was only one snag to this – the service along the most interesting branch-lines was so infrequent that if you weren't careful you could end up being marooned at places like Craven Arms or Market Drayton for the best part of a day, thus losing out on the value of the ticket. However, my new-found interest in photography often made this seem unimportant; I sometimes acted impulsively by jumping out of the train at a station which seemed to offer outstanding photographic potential.

Thus it was that I came to Arley. I had taken a train from Snow Hill at some ridiculously early hour (to get full value from the concession, dawn starts were essential) and found myself at Bewdley at a time when sensible folk are beginning breakfast. The line up the Severn Valley was always one of my favourites and so I boarded the train which was about to leave for Shrewsbury, intending to break the journey at Coalport where there was an interesting selection of old lines crossing our track.

But that was not to be. The three-coach train hauled by a scruffy Class 3 tank puffed gently along the wooded riverside. The landscape, bathed in the golden light of the September sun, looked particularly beautiful. I realised that if I was to prove my worth as a photographer then such rare opportunities had to be seized. When the train drew up at Arley station I was the only passenger to step down onto the deserted platform. A disgruntled porter waited by the gate to collect my ticket and was disappointed to see my Runabout pass. I asked him the way to the village and he looked at me with contempt. He pointed down the hill and muttered, 'You'll have to take the ferry,' before tramping back towards the signalbox.

I walked down the hill past the Harbour Inn and waved towards the ferry, which was on the opposite shore. Arley made a delightful picture with its cottages nestling below the church. An intriguing tower rose just behind that of the

The distinctive turrets of Arley Castle are clearly seen in this pre-war photograph

church itself. When he reached me I asked the stout, rosy-cheeked ferryman what it was, saying that it could make a creepy photograph.

'You're right, boy, Arley Castle is a funny old place, and you can only see half of it from here. It stands empty now and God alone knows what will become of it. The Woodwards lived there before the war and Lord Mount Norris before them. He was a real mean old beggar – the most hated man in Worcestershire. If you want to know about them you'd best look in the church.'

I walked up the hill to the church, which was beautiful and a haven of peace. There were numerous monuments, several of them commemorating tragic, untimely accidents. The oldest was a medieval effigy, at the east end of the church, which lay on the tomb of Sir Walter de Bahun. In 1270 he was summoned by King Henry III to take part in the eighth Crusade. At Southampton, where the Crusade was assembling, he married Isolda, the daughter of the Earl of Marche. In the tournament held to celebrate the wedding he was unhorsed and suffered injuries 'which shortly caused his death', as the church guide had it.

By the door of the church a plaque on the wall told of another honeymoon tragedy. This concerned Henry Arthur Annesley, Viscount Valentia (I had wondered why the hotel in the village was called the Valentia), who was the son of the first earl of Mount Norris. After thirteen days of marriage to Sarah Ainsworth he injudiciously bathed in the sea at Blackpool on 27 August 1818. The words on the plaque ended:

The circumstances attending his death were most affecting and awful. When bathing in the sea at Blackpool he was borne away by the violence of the waves. The vital spark was suddenly extinguished and his relatives plunged into the deepest distress.

Finally in this catalogue of tragedy there was another plaque, in the chancel, which told of the gallant death of Captain Robert Woodward in 1915. Although he had been wounded earlier in the day so severely that he could not bear arms, he insisted on leading his men in a charge from the trenches in 1915 and was killed as soon as they went over the top. We had been doing the Great War at school and I could imagine the horror of his death. After reading of these disasters it was a relief to leave the church.

The churchyard was a good viewpoint for Arley Castle, which was a splendid brick building in the Gothic style. Although I had been brought up not to trespass, its towers and battlements seemed to draw me towards them with some sort of magnetic force. Having been told the building was empty I persuaded myself that there could be little harm in my taking a photograph or two of it. When I drew closer I saw that the place was indeed abandoned, its ground-floor windows shuttered while those of the upper storeys had their curtains drawn. One window high up in a tower was broken and I thought for a moment that I saw movement there, but then concluded that the breeze must have stirred its curtain. Yet I still had the feeling of being watched – it was a creepy place to be alone.

For all this, the enormous castellated façade of the mansion held definite possibilities for a budding photographer and I began setting up my tripod, then rummaging in my haversack for an orange filter (a gimmick I was very attached to then; it would darken the sky dramatically on the black and white print).

My feeling of unease grew when I looked into the viewfinder. Suddenly my back felt vulnerable and the hairs on my neck prickled. There was a sudden rustling in the tangled rhododendrons just behind me, and turning suddenly I was sure I glimpsed a shadowy figure hurrying away.

I finished taking the picture, telling myself not to be such a cissie, and decided to look around the rest of the building. The great front door of dark oak was sheltered by a carriage porch and proved to be securely bolted. I walked round to the back, which seemed even creepier than the front. Sunshine would never reach these damp and dismal courtyards. The doors of outhouses stood half-open and I steeled myself to peer inside a couple of the buildings – they looked as though they had once served as dairy and laundry. I passed through an arch into an inner courtyard even gloomier than anything that had gone before, but ahead a door into the castle itself stood open, the passage beyond it leading into the interior of the building. I

'Broken Stillness' – an evocation of the days of steam in the Lake District with Bassenthwaite in the background

dared myself to enter, thinking that my self-respect would be saved if I ventured just a little way inside.

The first room off the passageway was the kitchen. This was a comparatively friendly place since it was light and airy – its height took in two storeys and the roof had a central skylight. It was a vast room with the Victorian cooking-range (which would be worth a fortune today) still intact.

Beyond the kitchen the passageway became dark but a hint of light could be seen at the end, where a door stood ajar. I reached this and saw that the light came from another skylight, which illuminated the main staircase, a masterpiece of elaborate woodcarving. The main rooms led off the stairway hall. Though bare of furniture these were magnificent in the sombre style of the early nineteenth century. Broken shutters added to the eerie atmosphere of the place, allowing pools of sunlight to fall on the dusty floor. In one of these lay a book, which I picked up. It was a Latin grammar, the inside of its cover carrying the book-label of Arley Hall Private School for Girls, with the name Nancy Fuller neatly written below. On its title-page someone had scrawled: 'I am a prisoner here, please let me out' – I hoped this was a joke.

I shivered; the pool of light became pale as the sun went behind a cloud. I felt that I had explored enough to satisfy my self-esteem, and began to retrace my footsteps towards the kitchen door. I was about to enter the passageway when I heard a voice behind me: 'Stay just where you are, I've got a gun.'

I stopped, frightened out of my wits, and turned slowly. There was a figure on the stairs and I thought that I could indeed make out the shadow of a gun. As I turned, however, the whole scene seemed to change as though it were being turned inside out. The dim, dusty, empty stairwell was suddenly transformed into a very different place where rich brocade curtained the windows and a deep crimson carpet covered the stairs and hallway. Now there was furniture, too – a long-case clock stood at the bottom of the stairs, and enormous Chinese vases held plants which had put forth an abundance of luxuriant fronds.

I only had seconds to take in this transformation before my attention was reclaimed by the man on the stairs. I could now see him perfectly clearly – an elderly man with cruel features, and dressed in the style of long ago. The gun he held was old-fashioned too, a blunderbuss with a flared, bell-shaped muzzle. The old man caught my glance. 'Yes,' he said, 'it's the gun I keep for house-breakers, and it's specially filled with shot that will cut you to pieces should you try anything foolish. Bring him to the business room, Phillips.'

I became aware of a man behind me, who pushed me forward. He too was holding a gun but was dressed in a more rustic way, in smock and gaiters. Glancing down at myself I found my usual grey flannels and open-necked shirt gone; instead I wore a thick, muddy greatcoat and heavy boots. The study was a book-lined room dominated by a large desk. A fire blazed in the grate and the atmosphere seemed almost unbearably stuffy. The cruel-faced man entered the room without his gun and sat down behind the desk. He looked at me severely through cold eyes which were deep-set in a sallow, wrinkled face. He had abundant but neatly trimmed whiskers. Phillips continued to stand behind me, his hand on my shoulder.

'You know now that we give short shrift to all who trespass at Arley, especially those who do so on behalf of the railway. I fear your master will never undertake another survey. A one-legged surveyor will be of little use to anyone, even if he is fortunate enough to recover.' The words were even more terrible for being spoken totally without emotion, but they seemed to strike a chord in my memory. I suddenly began to relive a nightmare.

I was in a wood, holding up a white post. Some distance away there was a man at a theodolite who waved his arms at me. Obediently I moved in the direction he indicated. He waved again and then began to walk towards me. At that moment he gave a scream and stumbled before falling head-long. He continued to scream, an agonised sound which set me running towards him. I found that his leg was held in the jaws of a vicious man-trap which had been concealed in the under-growth. Blood had already soaked through his trousers, which had been ripped by the serrated metal. I could see white slivers of bare bone amongst the torn flesh of the terrible wound. I wrestled with the trap but its spring was too strong,

Arley Station on the Severn Valley Railway has been lovingly restored

and I quickly realised that I was adding to his agony. His face was now ashen and his screams had dropped to a whimper; he spoke no words to me. I ran off to find help but had gone only a few yards when I came face to face with a group of grim-looking men. One of them grabbed me by the collar.

'Master'll be right pleased to see you,' he said, 'I'd best take you back to the hall.'

He looked at the others.

'You get the fellow out of the trap and take him to the surgeon. I doubt if he'll have any further use for that leg.'

My reverie was ended by the cruel-faced man's next words, which returned me to my present predicament in the study.

'You may tell your patrons, especially your precious Mr Nicholson, that the railway will not be coming through Arley and that's the finish of it. I have no time for railways and am not going to be dictated to on the matter by hypocrites like Whitmore, who cares to promote your railway to others but won't let it within sight of his own house at Apley.'

He turned to Phillips and spoke harshly: 'Give the boy the beating of his life and then set him loose – that should warn the beggars off.'

Phillips turned me towards the door and pushed me through it. I could see how much he would enjoy thrashing me and tried to think of some way of escape. As we approached the door to the kitchen passage, where the vision had started, the scene began to blur and then to turn itself inside out again. A great dizziness came over me and I stopped and leaned against the wall....

'I say, are you all right?'

I heard the words only dimly through the fog of my confusion. Again there was a figure on the stairs with a gun, but as he came towards me I saw, my dizziness now gone, that he was very unlike the man I had encountered there before. He too was elderly and had a fine set of whiskers, but his face was kindly and his eyes twinkled. He spoke again:

'Are you always as pale as this? I'm afraid I must have given you a fright, but I was after the scoundrels who've been taking the lead from the roof. They think they can do what they like with the place since it stands empty. What are you doing here, anyway?'

The last words came out almost apologetically, as though he didn't really want to find out why I was trespassing in the house. I stammered out my explanation. He smiled and sat himself down on the dusty stairs. Then he went on:

'I suppose my scaring the hell out of you serves you right for trespassing. Still, there's no harm done, though if you'd been caught trespassing at Arley a hundred years ago things might have gone differently. Lord Mount Norris used to tell his keepers to shoot on sight, you know, and made them put down traps against poachers. Once he got into trouble when he snared a fellow surveying for the railway – poor chap died too – but the old boy had plenty of friends in high places so in the end nothing came of it.'

He paused, and looked at me thoughtfully before continuing.

'On his deathbed, though, the surveyor cursed him, his offspring and all who lived in the castle. The old earl died soon after without a direct heir and my grandfather bought the estate. I believe the fortunes of our family changed when we came to Arley. They went downhill, not in a spectacular way but steadily. I've tried everything to keep the castle – even let it to a school, but that went bust. Now all it's good for is salvage, or so I've been told. The bank tells me there's a man in Wolverhampton who will buy it for its bricks and timber, but that will hardly pay for me to end my days in Kensington or Cheltenham. Still, I shouldn't burden you with my problems, young man, you'll want to be on your way.'

He rose briskly from his seat on the stairs, brushing dust from his trousers. We shook hands and I left by the back door.

The castle was demolished soon after but inevitably its memory endures in my mind. I often wonder what happened to that surveyor's apprentice. Sometimes I visit a place for the first time and know that I've been there before, though perhaps not in this existence. Nearly always these places have strong connections with railways and I like to think that the spirit of my *alter ego* – the surveyor's apprentice – enjoys visiting them just as I do.

The Severn Valley Railway is generally recognised as the premier private-enterprise standard-gauge railway in the UK, and has achieved its pre-eminent position through diligent attention to detail since it started scheduled steam-hauled passenger services from Bridgnorth to Hampton Loade in May 1970.

Now, over two decades later, the railway runs for sixteen miles from Bridgnorth beyond the original limit of services at Hampton Loade all the way to a purpose-built but traditionally constructed terminal station at Kidderminster, immediately adjacent to the BR station. Thus over 200,000 visitors a year can enjoy a splendidly scenic and authentically restored stretch of railway, with the chance to view the largest collection of operational steam locomotives and passenger coaches in the entire country.

To travel on the railway is not only to enjoy the exhilaration of seeing steam locomotives at work in sylvan surroundings, but also to see a complete railway in perspective, with traditional station buildings, imposing bridges, lovely old signal-boxes, and an impressive array of semaphore signals and telegraph poles stretching as far as the eye can see. Admiring members of the public are attended to professionally but personally by smartly attired uniformed staff who call to mind the imposing figures of the stationmasters of yesteryear. The whole enterprise manifests a vitality which is perhaps the most telling evidence of its success.

The Nightmare of Stefan Weiss

For the third night in succession Stefan Weiss woke from his nightmare screaming, and wet with the sweat of terror. His wife, Rita, was standing by his bed looking concerned. 'If you get another of these you'll be off to see the doctor,' she said. 'I'm not having you disturb my beauty sleep again. It's not as though you tell me what's up, anyway.'

Stefan had covered his eyes with hands which were still trembling. 'It's nothing,' he said, 'just a dream of the war.'

He had always been reticent on that subject, thought Rita, perhaps with good reason. Stefan had been some twenty years older than she when they married in 1962; she knew that he had been conscripted into the German army and had served through most of the war before surrendering to the British, but he had never told her much about his experiences. They had met when she had been a stewardess with BEA, and though the age-gap was wide the marriage had been relatively successful. Stefan's expertise in making money meant that they had been able to enjoy an affluent lifestyle, while his frequent absences on business left her with opportunities to cultivate companions of her own age and, in later years, even younger. She had raised two children, both of whom were launched on promising careers.

Meanwhile, lying on his bed, Stefan was reflecting on his dream. It was a very private one.

He recognised the event which had triggered the series of nightmares. Their daughter Tanya was a surgeon who was occasionally let down by baby-minders. When this happened Rita and Stefan took charge of the two young children. Just before Christmas an unexpected rush of work had left Tanya without cover for the children and she had telephoned her parents in desperation. They had eagerly accepted and decided to treat the grandchildren with a trip on the Santa Special operated by the Nene Valley Railway, which was close to their East Midlands home. They reserved seats for the Wednesday before Christmas and, arriving in good time at Wansford station, waited for the train to return from its previous trip. A bell rang, the crossing-gates closed across the road, and a column of smoke announced the arrival of the train as it curved its way towards them past the water-meadows.

It was then that the shock hit him. The locomotive was not to the usual British pattern. It seemed much larger than a normal engine with many of its pipes and working parts exposed to view outside its body, giving it a sinister appearance – a little like an anatomical drawing where the skin is stripped away to show the veins and muscles beneath. Immediately Stefan was transported back through time, to the freight-yard outside Warsaw where his infantry platoon were occupied in loading a pitiful human cargo into the cattle vans which would take them to the extermination camps.

At the time Stefan had hidden his shock at meeting the loco again. He was sure that it was identical to the one he remembered, and study of the literature on sale in the shop at

Wansford station – this building is reputed to be haunted though not by the ghost of Stefan Weiss

The Nene Valley Railway's 'Kriegslok' loco ready to haul a Santa Special

Wansford seemed to confirm this. Neither Rita nor the children noticed anything strange about him at the time, but the latter were too excited at the prospect of meeting Santa to take heed of other things. Once aboard the train Rita had glanced at him and asked if he was all right: she said he'd suddenly turned pale. Stefan ignored this and tried to behave normally, but the regular beat of wheels on rails brought back the dreadful images – the tortured faces of the mothers holding their babies, the haggard grandfathers who would have been about the age he was now, and above all the children with their stick-like limbs and their eyes enormous with apprehension.

He had lived with his guilt for fifty years and through that time had constantly rehearsed excuses to himself. After all, he had only been a humble foot-soldier then, the lowest of the low, and just twenty years old. But he had been there and done his share of the evil. He had heard the dilemma discussed a thousand times on radio and television and read thousands of words of condemnation, but only now, aboard a train hauled by a Polish locomotive and with his wife and grandchildren beside him, did the enormity of the Holocaust hit his spirit. His wife looked at him more sharply as she saw tears run down his leathery, wrinkled cheeks.

For a reason Stefan could not understand the railway drew him back. It seemed to offer an escape from the guilt which had been with him for so long. He needed only to see the imposing shape of the engine to feel relief, and soon joined the preservation society in the hope of getting even closer to the loco. He made no secret of his attachment to it and welcomed the chance to work on the more unpleasant chores, like cleaning its tubes and firebox, as a kind of penance. His ambition was to work on the footplate, and occasionally he was allowed a ride, but there was no shortage of younger men to act as firemen, so although he contributed generously to the loco's upkeep that particular ambition seemed thwarted.

Meanwhile his nightmares continued and grew in intensity. He refused Rita's incessant demands that he visit a doctor, psychiatrist, hypnotherapist. She moved out of the master bedroom and into the guest suite.

It proved harder for Stefan to find distraction in winter. Certainly there were mundane tasks to do on the railway but the Polish engine was seldom in steam, and increasingly it seemed that only a weird sort of communion with this piece of machinery could ease Stefan's torment of mind.

He turned to drugs for relief – barbiturates brought repose at night but the days were terrible. To combat this problem he began to drink heavily; this brought endless disputes with Rita who, after one quarrel, stormed out of the house to stay with her daughter. Eventually she told Tanya of the situation.

'It all started when we went to that bloody railway,' she said. 'Since then he's been living in some sort of hell but I've no idea what it is.'

'Short of getting him certified I don't think there's anything we can do,' her daughter replied. 'It's not as though he's a danger to anyone except himself.'

In fact Stefan was getting to be a menace to everyone. He was soon experimenting with cocktails of different drugs and drinking more heavily. It was easy for a man of his wealth to support such a habit. He still drove his Jaguar, visited the golf club, and attended masonic functions, but his friends were shocked at the change in him. His once stocky frame became shrunk and stooped so that he looked almost dwarf-like. His eyes were deeply sunk, his hands shook, and he was unable to keep up the most simple of conversations. However, he continued to reject all of his family's attempts to help. When his daughter consulted a mutual friend who was also in medicine they concluded that he had contracted a terminal illness which he was keeping secret from the family. 'I only hope he doesn't do anything silly,' the doctor said as they parted.

Two days after this conversation Stefan woke from a sixteen-hour drug-induced sleep feeling a different man. He now knew just what he had to do. He moved jerkily but with great power, bumping furniture out of the way. Clumsily he made his way to the garage and drove the Jaguar out, reversing until stopped by the impact with an ornamental statue. He drove to Wansford in maniacal style, but fortunately it was early on a Sunday morning and there was little traffic about. All the same, only good luck saved him from killing himself and at least a dozen other road-users.

At Wansford he parked the car close to the loco shed. The Polish tank was already out, having taken a track-laying train to Yarwell Junction. With a snort of disgust Stefan left the yard. Onlookers watched in amazement as he negotiated the points to get out onto the main line. He followed the trackwork just as a loco would, reversing to the closed crossing-gates before going up the main line towards the tunnel. As he passed the shed he gave a bellow which might have been meant to sound like a whistle. The spectators, who had grown in numbers, were now doubled up with laughter. 'He must have had a few last night,' said one.

'And this morning, too,' replied his mate. 'I bet he doesn't make it through the tunnel.'

Stefan managed to steam through the tunnel all right, though by then his pace had slowed and he was gasping for breath. The crew of the Polish tank had dropped their train at the far end of the track and were returning to Wansford for their breakfast. They saw the strange figure emerge from the tunnel and thought it must be a jogger, his elbows rhythmically jerking like pistons. They gave a warning blast of the whistle, but to no effect. The runner kept to his course plumb in the middle of the track without changing speed. The driver closed the regulator and frantically screwed down the brake, swearing violently as he did so. At the last moment he threw over the reversing lever and sparks flew as the driving wheels changed direction. To no avail: the runner seemed oblivious and was still running in the same manner, elbows pumping up and down, when he was struck by the buffer beam. There was no sound other than hissing steam and screaming metal as he collided with the loco. The small snow-plough in front of the bogies saved him from being killed outright, but he suffered terrible injuries from being pushed along the track, and died before reaching hospital. Yet his bloodied face was bearing a triumphant smile as they lifted him onto the stretcher. He spoke just five enigmatic words before losing consciousness. 'I can face God now,' he said.

The Nene Valley Railway has been rebuilt almost from scratch. The last scheduled passenger services were run by British Railways in 1966, though occasional freight trains and specials used the track through Wansford until 1972. Soon after this the Nene Valley Railway Society was formed and began restoring the former LNWR line.

Today this reaches eastwards to Peterborough itself, and westwards through Wansford tunnel to Yarwell Junction, where the Rugby and Northampton lines once divided.

A unique feature of the Nene Valley line is the opportunity it gives to see British and continental locos and rolling-stock being worked side by side.

To forestall pundits who will point to inaccuracies, the engine featured in our story and which resides at Wansford was not, in fact, manufactured in Poland nor is it likely that it was there when the exodus from the Warsaw ghettoes took place. The 'Kriegslok' locomotive was built in Vienna in 1943 and worked mainly from Dresden until the end of the war. Then it was confiscated by the USSR and worked in Russia until 1959, when it was bought by the Polish State Railways. It came to Wansford in 1989.

'Day's End' – a painting of the Midland Railway south of Loughborough